ON THE ROAD WITH JESUS

On the Road With Jesus

DAVE CAPE
WITH **DOUG LAURIE**

STRUIK CHRISTIAN BOOKS

———————

KINGSWAY PUBLICATIONS

EASTBOURNE

Unless otherwise indicated, biblical quotations are from the
New American Standard Bible © The Lockman Foundation
1960, 1962, 1963, 1968, 1971, 1972, 1973.

ISBNs
0 85476 369 4 (Kingsway)
1 86823 171 2 (Struik Christian Books)

Struik Christian Books Ltd
(A member of the Struik Publishing Group (Pty) Ltd)
Cornelis Struik House
80 McKenzie Street
Cape Town 8001
South Africa

Reg. No. 04/02203/06

Produced by Bookprint Creative Services
P.O. Box 827, BN23 6NX, England for
KINGSWAY PUBLICATIONS LTD
Lottbridge Drove, Eastbourne, E Sussex BN23 6NT
Printed in Great Britain by Clays Ltd, St Ives PLC
Typeset by J&L Composition Ltd, Filey, North Yorkshire

Dedication

To my beloved wife Carol,
my daughter Carynne
and my son Ronnie-Russ
with whom I have laughed, cried and dreamed.
Together we have walked.
Together we have kept the faith,
in joy and sorrow, in victory and despair.
Together we have experienced, lived and seen
the truth and faithfulness of our wonderful God,
and of his precious Son, Jesus.

Contents

Preface

This is the challenging story of David's experiences as he travels South Africa and beyond, washing the feet of many well-known and lesser known people. No matter who they are, high profile or not, no matter what age or race, everyone whose feet David washes is touched by God. David's intimate relationship with the Lord shines through the pages in his conversations with God and the way in which he takes God's word literally and obeys.

Starting in Soweto, where his life was on the line, he walked more than three thousand kilometres through Natal, the Transkei and the Eastern Cape to Cape Town, carrying a load of over 20kgs (45lbs) in extremes of weather conditions and encountering many hardships. He has had meetings with Heads of State, with mayors of major cities and army generals. He tells how after his South African journey, he and his family settled back in their Randburg home, yet at the end of 1990, he felt God's call for him to go to the Middle East. Subsequently his ministry took him into the middle of the Gulf War.

David's simple trust in the Lord led him to take a step of faith which resulted in his seeing God at work in the lives of the people of South Africa and beyond. He continues to make this prophetic statement of the servant love of Jesus as he carries the cross and bowl in the nations of the world.

Ray McCauley
Rhema Bible Church
Randburg, South Africa

Foreword

The sociological upheavals which are taking place in South Africa are generally presented by the media as fruits of political negotiations and pressures: very little is ever mentioned of what is going on behind the scenes. I do not mean the political, economic or sociological manoeuvrings which plague most power struggles or pursuits of justice; rather I refer to the supernatural and spiritual background against which all of world history is enacted.

Many individual Christians, black, white, coloured, Asian, of all denominations have been involved at a hidden and therefore an inevitably and predictably overlooked level, leavening society, just as Jesus promised his followers they would if they lived in obedience to him (Mt 13:33). This takes faith, as Jesus clearly implies, and it challenges us to expect that ordinary people can be the leaven of change or, to use another of his metaphors, salt and light in society, as he commands (Mt 5:13ff). How can the ordinary man, distanced from the means of power and tables of decision make an impression for good in a society?

We have in this book the story of one man of faith whose obedience and persistence have contributed to that supernatural changing of a society which outwardly appeared to be either beyond change or, at the very least, open to change only through violence and bloodshed. The extent by which the expected violence has been averted must be because of many such people as David Cape who have followed their Lord in faith.

11

The story of David's sacrificial obedience, paid for by himself and his family, is told in these enthralling chapters. His story must be one among many of Christian lives of faith and commitment which have contributed to the immense changes in South Africa. Having read this book we have to ask God, as David did, 'What do you want *me* to do, Lord?' and expect, along with David, to hear God's specific answers. These may be beyond anything we could have imagined, but we need to step out obediently into the adventure, the creativity and the surprises of walking with Jesus.

We have known David and Carol as friends over a number of years, and have had the privilege of their ministry in our Ichthus Christian Fellowship in London. It has also been our pleasure to meet other folk who are mentioned in the book. Our commendation is that the wonderful record of David and Carol's obedience and the unlikely interventions of God into their lives is just the sort of story we would expect from people of their integrity.

In actual fact, David's unique account is drawing on a theme which the Spirit of God is revealing among God's people throughout the world: namely the thrusting of Christians out of buildings on to the streets; taking the walls off the church to show what the church really is—people full of the love and compassion of Jesus. It is a movement out from the church to the people instead of a passive waiting for people to come to the church. 'March for Jesus', prayer-walking the streets of our cities, towns and villages, prayer journeys—these are all facets of this theme, from which David has drawn, and into which he has also contributed.

Miraculous escapes, angelic intervention, signs and wonders following the preaching of the word, all show that the Acts of the Apostles is still being written.

What would be the result if the hidden numbers of ordinary Christians worldwide were to rise to the challenge of this extraordinary story? After all, we do have an extraordinary Saviour! Surely the coming of the kingdom of God would be hastened and the world's perception of the people of God would be transformed—and certainly a few more of David's and the world's Goliaths would fall!

Roger Forster
Ichthus, London

Route followed by Dave Cape through Southern Africa.
(Indicated by ·············)

1

Soweto

'I must be crazy. Do I really want to do this? Will people actually let me wash their feet? Lord,' I said, half aloud, 'I feel such a fool. Why don't you open the ground and swallow me, and let's just pretend this never happened?'

These and similar thoughts came thick and fast as I trudged along the litter-laden street that morning, breathing in the smoggy residue of Soweto's coal fires. Clad in shorts, a T-shirt printed with 'Jesus-washed feet are happy feet', thick rubber-soled walking shoes, rolled-down hiking socks and with a large contraption on my back, I made quite a spectacle, even by Soweto's relaxed standards. The contraption contained large water tanks, Bibles, towels which read 'Washed clean by Jesus', a small camping chair and a wooden cross and bowl. Inconspicuous it wasn't.

'Lord, I feel such a fool,' I said again.

'David,' I sensed the voice of the Holy Spirit saying in reply, 'I want you to look like this because I want you to be my witness.'

I have since come to realise that if I have to be a fool, I would rather be a fool for Jesus than for anyone else. The world already has enough fools of its own. But on that chilly October morning everything was still ahead of me, unknown, threatening.

With my knees knocking I walked three blocks, attracting curious stares from passers-by. Virtually no whites are seen in Soweto; only a small percentage of white Johannesburg residents have ever entered it. The township, as it was formerly known, is located south-west of Johannesburg (hence the name Soweto). A vast, sprawling conglomerate of dwellings ranging from shanties to palatial residences, it is home to almost three million people.

It is a city where human life is cheap. Illegitimacy rates are high, with perhaps 70% of babies born out of wedlock. The result is a savage harvest of troubled children, frequently seeking violence as a solace to the apparent pointlessness of life. An average weekend in Soweto yields some five to ten murders and as many rapes, although it is believed that many more of the latter go unreported. Born out of an evil apartheid system, Soweto's ills are compounded by widespread demon worship. There are estimated to be at least three thousand practising witch doctors in Soweto, and Christianity is often seen as 'the white man's religion'.

At the time when I began my walk, Soweto was simmering with unusual unrest. 'Necklace' murders were commonplace. A victim would be forced to stand with a car tyre round his neck, and the inner part of the tyre would be filled with petrol. He would then be given a box of matches and ordered to set himself alight. A cruel death from burning and suffocation would ensue as the crowds danced and jeered around the spectacle.

This was the place where I had felt impelled by God to begin my long pilgrimage across Southern Africa, and it was a real baptism of fire in its own way for me. Less than a minute into my faltering journey, I noted four extremely rough-looking gangster types saunter across the road towards me. At that moment I felt anything but God's man of faith and power.

'What do you want here?' the ringleader demanded aggressively.

Part of the preparation for my trip had been getting bright fluorescent 'I'm walking with Jesus' stickers printed. As a conversational ice-breaker I began sticking these on the gangsters, muttering, 'You've got to get stuck up with Jesus.' It wasn't very good theology, but it was all I could think of at the time. Once I had regained my composure, I started to tell them about the love of Jesus, how he had died for them, paid the price for all their sins and how nothing they had ever done could override the price paid on the cross. After twenty minutes, I asked them if they had understood and if they would like to receive Jesus into their hearts. The answer was yes, much to my joy. I said, 'If you are embarrassed, we can go and pray somewhere else.'

'No,' they responded, 'we want to pray right here.' So there on the streets of Soweto, within the first half hour of my being on the road, I witnessed God's faithfulness as these four gangsters surrendered their hearts to the living God. It was to prove a significant event. As the four turned to go, a most beautiful thing occurred, which has never again happened to me. One of them said to the other three, 'You go. I am following this man.' I had an inkling of how Jesus must have felt as James and John, the sons of Zebedee, left their father mending the nets and immediately followed him.

The man's name was Peter, and I believe God provided him to protect me. He rapidly gained a thorough understanding of Scripture as, interpreting for me, he preached the gospel at least fifty times in the next two days. Formerly a notorious gangster, Peter was well-known throughout the township. Once I had finished washing feet, he would go out to hang the towels on the fence and tip the water out of the bowl. People would then frequently whisper conspiratorially to me, 'It's good that Peter is with you; he needs to hear these things that you are preaching.' On more than one occasion, when a hostile crowd gathered to jeer and mock, Peter would show them his fist, and silence would instantly reign. Not exactly perfect Christian behaviour perhaps, but effective in the circumstances nevertheless.

From the outset, I have always known God's faithfulness—but I know, too, that he constantly checks out my obedience. Had I backed off that very first day, the thousands upon thousands who have come to know

Jesus while they had their feet in the bowl would never have known the saving grace of our Lord. The first day I was out on the streets of Soweto, the Holy Spirit allowed me to lead sixteen people to the Lord and wash thirteen pairs of feet. The next day, it was thirteen people led to the Lord and sixteen pairs of feet washed. That night God spoke to me. 'David, I do not want you to keep count of how many feet you wash and how many people come to salvation, because I never want you to start striving, only to be obedient to what I show you.'

I don't know how many feet we have washed by now along the highways and byways, only that it is many thousands, and God has taught me that there is no success or failure in the kingdom of God, only obedience. Does it make it a successful day when I wash twenty or thirty pairs of feet? Am I a failure when I wash none at all? I don't think so. God looks on the heart, and all that he desires and seeks of us is that we obey him as faithful children.

Some days in Soweto were truly glorious days with God. I found the people at times so spontaneous and such an encouragement to me as a white man whom they would have had every right to despise. The people of Diepkloof (a suburb of Soweto) in particular, were so kind. They fed me, greeted me and would wave to me on the streets.

One morning as I walked some way into Diepkloof, a younger woman approached me and asked if I would come to her house, where she introduced me to her mother and then rounded up the whole neighbourhood. The little house was jam-packed as I shared the love of Jesus with the people, and then after inviting people to receive Jesus as Lord, I began washing their feet. It was a marathon that lasted about two-and-a-half hours. Next, a dear man from across the road asked me to go to his house. I went in and there again the lounge was full. Another marathon! Towards the end of that day, people were sending messengers to call me into their homes, saying, 'Please tell the man with the cross and bowl to

Washing feet

come to pray for us and to wash our feet.' It was like walking with Jesus.

At one stage during the day I went into a place which unbeknown to me was a shebeen (an illegal drinking house) and after sharing the gospel with the folk sitting around drinking, I had the joy of leading the shebeen 'Queen' to Jesus before all her clientele as I washed four people's feet and saw them all come to salvation. God is so marvellous. Praise his name!

One Saturday morning, to my delight, a black pastor friend of mine announced that he and a couple of others were going to accompany me on my round throughout Soweto. We had decided to take a long walk down one of the main roads running through the centre of Diepkloof towards Orlando, but we hadn't gone far when I stopped to talk to a young man. Soon he was joined by three others. We had a lovely time sharing the gospel with the four of them as a large crowd began to gather. After a while we managed to lead them to salvation, whereupon I began washing their feet. The street became incredibly busy as bystanders continued to crowd around. Cars began to stop and people in nearby houses were amazed at the sight. After washing the feet of the four men we gave them gospel literature, and there was great jubilation. The people were coming out of their houses thanking me for coming to Soweto and for bringing the love of Jesus to them. Shortly after that, another lady came and said that she did not know Jesus, but would like to know him. I very willingly shared the gospel with her, and had the privilege of seeing her come to salvation, and washed her feet on the pavement.

Next we entered another house, where people came in one after the other and we started seeing them come to salvation, thereafter washing their feet. It was a real privilege. My companions said that they hadn't realised how powerful this ministry was, and even though I felt like a real spectacle at times, I thanked God for glorifying himself in Soweto.

During this time, God began to teach me much about obedience to him, and I started to ponder on how God has always only been able to use those who are obedient to him. Abraham, I reflected, was just such a man. At the age of seventy-five, at the command of God, he uprooted everything to move to 'the land which I will show you' (Gen 12:1). Then when he finally arrived in Canaan, the Promised Land, God moved him on once again into the wilderness. Time and again, we see how God checked out Abraham's obedience, and each time only as Abraham was obedient to do things in God's way was God able to honour him. The ultimate test of Abraham's obedience was his willingness to offer his only son back to God as a sacrifice. It came to the point of Abraham's knife being upraised above Isaac, his precious son, before God stopped him, saying, 'I know now that you fear God.'

Because of Abraham's obedience, God said to him,

> I will make you the father of a multitude of nations . . . By Myself I have sworn, declares the Lord, because you have done this thing, and have not withheld your son, your only son, indeed I will greatly bless you, and I will greatly multiply your seed as the stars of the heavens . . . And in your seed all the nations of the earth shall be blessed, because you have obeyed My voice (Gen 22:17–18).

Had it not been for Abraham's obedience to God, there would have been no Isaac, no Jacob, no Joseph, no continuation of the messianic bloodline down through David ultimately to Jesus. And if there had been no Jesus, you and I would not have been able to live in the fulness of the victory of the cross of Jesus to this day. It amazes me to think that one man's obedience changed the course of history. I often wonder how many Abrahams are walking around today in disobedience to God, missing out on the enormous potential that he would release through them if only they would listen, trust and obey.

During my time in Soweto I acquired an entourage

that would go with me from house to house, and often I would get messages saying, 'Please ask the man with the cross and bowl to come.' More often than not these were requests to pray for healing, and one such request came from a lady who had heard that I was in the area, and asked me to come and pray for her mother-in-law. I arrived late in the day to find one of the most tragic sights I have ever seen. The situation in the house was one of abject poverty, with dirt everywhere and a stench pervading the entire place. There was almost no furniture and the kitchen was filthy. I have been in many broken-down, derelict places, but this must rank as one of the worst.

I was taken to a room where they had placed a dear old lady on a chair to await my arrival. I was told that there was a problem with her legs. She removed the blankets from her legs and feet, and the sight that greeted me was quite horrible. I have never seen such rotten legs and feet. Pus and blood were oozing out and running down. Her feet were swollen beyond recognition and the gangrenous sores were too terrible to describe. The only way to tell that her feet were in fact feet, was that they had toenails attached to the end.

I felt her greatest need was for spiritual help. Even though she was very old. I sensed there was some unforgiveness in her life. This turned out to be true, as apparently in her youth she had attacked and stabbed someone and had borne the hatred for the rest of her life. While I was ministering to her they had covered up her legs again, and she then complained that there was something bothering them, at which we discovered that a little puppy had run into the room and had started licking the sores. There was so much blood oozing from her legs that when they pulled the puppy away it was covered with blood and mucus. Once we had asked her to release the sins of her past to the Lord, I lifted her feet and placed them in the bowl and washed them. As I removed the bowl I saw that where her feet had been, a pool of blood had run down as she had been sitting talking to me. I have never in all my life felt so stretched on faith. As I was praying for the lady, I sensed the Lord saying to me, 'As you have done it for the least of these, you have done it for me.'

I would like to tell you that the lady was healed, but when I last heard, she wasn't, and I felt that the Lord was teaching me to trust him in obedience even when I didn't know why. He was instructing me to trust his word and to cling to the words of Jesus, 'Truly, truly, I say to you, he who believes in Me, the works that I do shall he do also, and greater works than these shall he do; because I go to the Father' (Jn 14:12). Through many tears and much persistence, simply clinging to that word over a period of time, I was able to see its truth worked out in my own life.

I remember one occasion of total humiliation while walking through the streets of Ladysmith in Natal. I came across a blind begger who was obviously well-known to the locals. As he sat on the pavement in front of me I felt my faith growing. I asked him to take off the very black spectacles that he wore. As I looked down at him, all I could see where the whites of his eyes rolling in their sockets. By this time a rather large crowd had gathered as they saw me standing over him with the cross and bowl. I placed my hands on his eyes and begged God to heal him, claiming the healing power of the Holy Spirit. As I removed my hands the whites of his eyes continued just to roll before me. The crowd laughed and mocked as I walked down the street weeping, not understanding, but trusting God's word that one day, somehow greater things than these would we do.

During these times when God continued to test me to see if I would serve him in obedience even when I didn't know why, I began to realise that God is also a God of encouragement. He continued to drop little nuggets of encouragement that would build my faith. For example, one afternoon during my time in Soweto I washed the feet of a dear old Zulu lady. She told me that she had come up to Soweto because of the extreme faction fights in Tugela in Natal. She later sought me out and said that before I had washed her feet she had had chronic diarrhoea and dreadful cramps in her stomach for several days, but that at the moment that I had washed her feet, the cramps had left her, and her stomach had settled down. Praise be to our God, who is indeed the God of all encouragement.

If we are to see the kingdom of God built, with the signs and wonders following that we read about in the Gospels and Acts, the starting point has to be simple obedience to that quiet inner voice of the Lord. For me the greatest single test of my obedience and faith came unannounced one morning in Soweto. I was walking alone through what I later heard was one of the most dangerous parts of the township, a haunt of all the worst gangsters, murderers, car thieves and bank robbers. A man—a gangster it subsequently transpired—was leaning on an iron gate with two friends. On approaching him, I stuck one of my fluorescent green 'I'm walking with Jesus' stickers on him and began engaging him in conversation. His two friends first pretended not to listen, but as the conversation hotted up they gradually became drawn in despite themselves, much to my inner amusement. After some time they conferred among themselves in their own language and then said to me, 'Come with us; we want to show you something.'

I felt the first prickle of an indefinable fear as I walked with them round to the back of the squalid building. 'Something' proved to be a small corrugated iron shed. At that moment, four other gangsters appeared, bringing the total to seven. Suddenly they hustled me into the shed and bolted the door closed from the inside. They crowded mockingly around me and began to jostle me in the small gloomy enclosure, some behind, some in front. My heart began to pound in my chest. I could feel myself breaking out in a cold sweat. I was unarmed, defenceless; they almost certainly carried knives. Even if I had been armed, there was no way I could have used a weapon in Jesus' name.

While all this was happening almost as if in slow motion, my mind was racing. So this was how it was going to end. And I had only just started. What about my dear wife Carol? My precious children? I was trapped, utterly alone. No way out. Just the smell of dust and close-up human sweat, as jeering and laughing my executioners moved in for the kill.

In that instant, a portion of Scripture dropped into my consciousness. It was from the Book of Revelation, and referred to God's people: '. . . they did not love their life even to death' (Rev 12:11). At once, I sensed that Jesus was asking me the profoundest of questions, the ultimate test of obedience: 'Do you love me enough to die for me?' And at that moment I knew in my innermost being that the answer was 'Yes' . . . that it would be far better to die in obedience, doing what God had called me to do, than to die in disobedience outside his will. All this happened in mere seconds as my assailants closed in on me. At any moment I expected the thrust of a knife. The incongruity of it battered my mind. I, who could have been sitting comfortably in my pastor's office in northern Johannesburg, was about to be murdered in a dingy backyard Soweto shed. How had I come to be here?

How?

2

You Want Me to Do What, *Lord?*

'However did you get into a ministry of footwashing?'

I have been asked that question many times since I have been on the road for Jesus. My reply is quite simple: 'I preached myself into it.'

It all started early one morning as I was reading from Luke's Gospel, chapter 4, verse 18, where Jesus said,

> The Spirit of the Lord is upon Me, because He anointed Me to preach the gospel to the poor. He has sent Me to proclaim release to the captives, and recovery of sight to the blind, to set free those who are downtrodden, to proclaim the favourable year of the Lord.

I was so strongly convicted by this word, that I was prompted to go a few Sundays later and preach on this theme to our home church in Robinhills, Randburg. The challenge to the folk at Church of the Nations that night was, 'Is the Spirit of the Lord really upon you?'

We were a church that claimed to be a Spirit-filled people, living in the fulness of the power of God's provision within the Holy Spirit, but it struck me that, if these were the criteria for God's Spirit to be upon his Son, then how much more upon us? Were we as a church really preaching the gospel to the poor? Were we truly proclaiming relief to the captives, those in spiritual bondage who were slaves to sin? Were we truly healing the sick in the way that Jesus desired and required us to do, and were we bringing hope to the outcasts and downtrodden in society? Were we truly evangelising and proclaiming the saving power of Jesus and his kingdom? We liked to think we were, but were we really doing these things, or were we just thinking and talking about them?

That night in the meeting there was a truly powerful move of God and his Holy Spirit and we saw much repentance and deliverance from bondage. As I drove home afterwards, I had a deep awareness of the two dynamics of the kingdom of God working in my heart at the same time. On one hand there was a sense of life and resurrection over what had taken place within the meeting that night; on the other hand there was a feeling of death and heaviness. I knew clearly that, within my own life, there was a whole area of my relationship with the Father that was not under the control of his Spirit. This set me on a whole new path in prayer, one that was destined to change my life. Each morning for the next month I would come back to the same verse in Luke 4. For an entire month, I did not read another verse and I said, 'Lord, I will not leave this place until this scripture is worked within my life.' Each day I would cry out to God, often with tears, pleading with him to let no part of my life or being remain outside his will, that I wanted the fulness of all that his Spirit had to offer and that I would leave no spiritual stone unturned until that was accomplished.

Then one morning, while praying in my lounge, I sensed the Lord directing me to verse 21 of Luke 4, 'Today, this scripture has been fulfilled in your hearing.' It was as if God was saying, 'All right, my son, this scripture is worked in you by my Spirit; it is yours.' Instantly I felt as if a huge weight had been lifted off me. I leapt around the lounge, dancing and praising God. But I knew in fact that this was not the end; it was only the beginning.

My immediate response was, 'Thank you for that, Father—but what happens now?' Over the next few weeks as I waited on the Lord, he directed me to John 2:5 where Jesus' mother said to the servants, 'Whatever

He says to you, do it.' That little verse stung me into action. I cried out to God, covenanting to do whatever he told me without compromise. Then I went back to the local church and preached, saying to them, '"Whatever He says to you, do it."' I said to the church that from now on whatever God told us to do, we were going to do. I think the Lord must have looked down and smiled at that moment and said, 'If only you knew what lies ahead.'

The next question was, 'But how will I know what to do, Lord?' to which I sensed him saying, 'See what I did and do it.' So with new spiritual eyes and ears, I began to read the Gospels afresh. For several months, I devoured the Gospels with much excitement and fervour, seeing the things that Jesus did and said. It was like fresh manna from heaven, as though I was standing on tiptoe to see what would happen next. Then one day like a bolt out of the blue, I was struck by John 13:4–5, a passage that was to shake every ounce of security that I had ever had, and change the course of my destiny here on earth.

> Jesus rose from supper, and laid aside His garments; and taking a towel, girded Himself about. Then He poured water into the basin, and began to wash the disciples' feet, and to wipe them with the towel with which He was girded (Jn 13:4–5).

I was awestruck at this act of the servant-love of Jesus. I suddenly had a vivid picture of Queen Elizabeth going down into the kitchens at Buckingham Palace and beginning to wash the feet of the servants there and how their reaction would be one of utter amazement. Then the Father said to me, 'You see, David, she is only an earthly monarch, but my Son is the King of kings and the Lord of lords.' I started crying as I sensed the selflessness of this beautiful act of our Lord. 'What are you actually saying to me, Lord?' I asked, and immediately sensed him reply, 'David, I want you to do that.'

'Fine, Lord,' I replied. 'I will do it, but to whom?', thinking it might be my wife Carol. She has nice clean feet. But the Lord asked me: 'When I trod this earth, where was my ministry, David?'

I paused and answered, 'In the streets with the people, Lord.'

He said, 'That's what I want you to do.'

'You want me to do *what*, Lord?' My eye then fell on verses 14 and 15 of that same passage from John 13, 'If I then, the Lord and the Teacher, washed your feet, you also ought to wash one another's feet. For I gave you an example that you also should do as I did to you.'

Have you ever wondered how Moses must have felt as he stood before the burning bush, his mind racing as he struggled to accept what God was telling him? I think I can identify a bit with him because that is very much how I felt when I began to realise what the Lord was saying. In fact, right then, I was trying to blow out the bush, but it wouldn't be extinguished. Filled with the same disbelief that Moses must have felt, I said, 'Lord, please confirm this to me through your Scriptures.' Immediately he reminded me of this verse:

> How then shall they call upon Him in whom they have not believed? And how shall they believe in Him whom they have not heard? And how shall they hear without a preacher? And how shall they preach unless they are sent? (Rom 10:14-15)

It was like being hit over the head with a baseball bat. If the Lord had spoken to me audibly it could not have been more clear. I received this as a major confirmation of what the Lord was saying to me in the light of the Great Commission.

I said, 'OK, Jesus, where do I start?'

'Right here with your own family,' replied the Lord.

My wife Carol had sensed God working deeply in my heart and life over the past few months. I would begin to see or read things and find myself weeping in the presence of the Lord. She later told me how touched

The family in 1992

and blessed she had been as she had seen the Lord dealing with me and softening my heart. I gathered my little family together in the lounge of our Randburg home: Carol, our fourteen-year-old daughter Carynne and our eleven-year-old son, Ronnie-Russ. As I began to share and pray and wash their feet, it was as if a bolt of lightning struck us from heaven. We all started sobbing uncontrollably and knew that there was something far bigger than ourselves at work.

The idea of going out on to the streets and washing people's feet was still bothering me, however. I was part of the pastoral team in my church in Robinhills, and it was far more comfortable to be a respectable pastor in the respectable northern suburbs of Johannesburg. We loved the people in the church. Carol and I were blessed and fulfilled in our roles within the life of Church of the Nations. What would people think? This was such an unusual thing. I ran the risk of people thinking that I had become odd or totally flipped out. Then the Lord reminded me, 'David, you covenanted with me to do whatever I told you to do.'

'OK, Lord,' I said, 'where to next?'

'Right here in your own back yard,' was his reply. We had had a black family living there for the past eleven years. I swallowed hard and called them in, sharing the gospel with them and washing their feet in the name of Jesus.

'What next, Lord?'

'I want you to go to the church and wash the feet of all those whom you serve.'

I had always had a deep desire for us as a church to be a praying people. So I stood up in church the next Sunday and announced that if anyone wanted to pray at any time of the day or night, I would be at the church to pray with them. I then took my sleeping bag, headed down to the church and for several days and nights we had a time of prayer revival. As the people came in their droves, I would pray with them and wash their feet in obedience to what God was saying. At one o'clock one

morning with many having to go to work later that day,
the prayer room at the church was crowded. After
several days and nights of experiencing the presence of
the Lord, we ended with a glorious time of praise and
worship on the final night. Having been obedient to the
Lord in this matter, my next question was: 'What now,
Lord?'

'I want you to go and tread the streets of Soweto for
ten days, washing feet and proclaiming "the favourable
year of the Lord".' Once again I started to do the Moses
wriggle, because things were now starting to get a little
hot. I said, 'Fine, Lord, I will consider that.' And the
Lord replied, 'David, you said you'd do whatever I told
you to do.'

'OK, Lord,' I said. But I sensed that there was still a
lot more in store.

One morning while I was speaking to the Father, I
asked, 'Where to after Soweto, Lord?' He suddenly
showed me the two capitals of our nation: Pretoria and
Cape Town. I sensed him saying, 'I want you to move
on foot through the streets, along the highways and
byways of this land, washing the people's feet and
sharing my love with them as you go.' I knew that I
really needed the Lord to confirm this. Almost a year
had elapsed since the Lord first started calling me, and
the work that he was doing in my life was so deep that
it had taken three months before I was even able to share
with Carol the things that he was saying. I had asked
her after those three months to begin praying about this
unusual thing that God was calling us to. In her usual
gracious way, she agreed to do so.

As I waited and prayed over the next months, the
confirmation came once again from Hebrews 12:12,
'Therefore, strengthen the hands that are weak.'

'What does that mean?' I asked, and sensed the Lord
saying in reply, 'As you go you will need strong hands
because you have much to carry.' The verse went on to
say, 'Strengthen the knees that are feeble.' I asked, 'And
that, Lord?'

His reply was, 'As you kneel to wash the nations' feet, you will need strong knees.' Verse 13 continues, 'And make straight the paths of your feet so that the limb which is lame may not be put out of joint, but rather healed.'

I asked, 'And what is that lame limb, Lord?'

His response was, 'You remember all those months ago, when I started working in your life, and you said that there was a whole area of your life that my Spirit was not upon?'

'Yes, Lord.'

'That is the limb that is lame within your life, and if you are disobedient I will put it right out of your life.'

Verse 15 goes on to say, 'See to it that no one comes short of the grace of God.' And even now as I tread the highways and byways, I greet in the name of the Lord, every single person I pass, whether he be on foot or in a motor vehicle, seeing to it that no one comes short of the grace of God.

I knew that God was honing me. I knew I was coming to the place of total surrender and found myself praying God's word back to him as he was etching his word upon the tablets of my heart. As I prayed scripture back to God, I knew once again that I was making a fresh covenant with him.

> Strengthen me according to Thy word. Remove the false way from me, and graciously grant me Thy law. I have chosen the faithful way; I have placed Thine ordinances before me. I cleave to Thy testimonies; O LORD, do not put me to shame! I shall run the way of Thy commandments, for Thou wilt enlarge my heart. Teach me, O LORD, the way of Thy statutes, and I shall observe it to the end. Give me understanding, that I may observe Thy law, and keep it with all my heart. *Make me walk* in the path of Thy commandments for I delight in it (Ps 119:28–35).

So, consistently throughout those fourteen months and beyond them, God faithfully through many diverse and wonderful means continued to confirm the call that he had given us as a family. One morning while praying, some months before we finally headed out, I had a vivid picture of my cross and bowl as it now looks. I had been looking at metal bowls in the shops, wondering which one to buy, but that morning I clearly felt the Lord showing me that the cross and bowl were to be of wood and not plastic and metal. I have no claims to being an artist, but I grabbed a pen and paper and quickly sketched the vision of the cross and bowl that I saw before me. Then on our days off Carol and I set about going to every place we knew that made or sold wooden bowls. We were faced with a two-fold problem: first, most wooden bowls taper very sharply and you are unable to get two feet into them. Secondly, carved wooden bowls in South Africa are fairly expensive, their price being approximately 10% of my monthly income at the time.

In the weeks and months that followed we searched high and low, but to no avail. Then one day, while out in the country at a little village called Magaliesberg, we walked into a tiny shop and there was the bowl. It closely fitted the description the Lord had given me. Excitedly, I dug my hand into my pocket, only to feel Carol tugging on my arm, saying, 'No, wait. The Lord will give you the bowl that he wants you to have.' With my emotions whirling, and feeling a mixture of frustration and also despair, I said, 'If we do not do what the Lord tells us to do now, he is going to give it to someone else to do.' Something in my wife's clear, gentle stare, however, pulled me up short. Like an obedient submissive husband, I sheepishly put the money back into my pocket and the two of us emerged from the shop empty-handed. While all this was going on, we held this call close to our hearts, not yet sharing it even with our fellow elders and pastors at the church in Robinhills.

During this time a young couple from our church, whose marriage service I had been privileged to conduct, had gone on honeymoon to Malawi, a small neighbouring African country, several thousand kilometres to the north. One Sunday morning at church after their return, they informed me that they had a gift in their car for me. After the service, we went to the car park where they produced a most exquisite hand-carved ebony bowl, the carving depicting two people helping to lift one another's loads. I think the young couple felt a little embarrassed about giving a man a wooden bowl, but I was so excited that I said to them, 'Just lay your hands on this bowl and pray over it; it is the most beautiful gift I have ever received.'

The next task was the construction of the cross, which to many a do-it-yourself handyman might seem a minor detail. My wife declares that the fact that I built the cross myself must surely be the confirmation of the Lord and a miracle of the Holy Spirit. I am so unhandy, that if I knock a nail into a piece of wood, invariably the nail bends and the wood splits. Praise the Lord, the cross was finally constructed and the bowl mounted on it.

People sometimes talk about me carrying a cross, but I always say to them I carry a bowl that just happens to be attached to a cross. The reason the bowl is mounted on a cross is that so often I go into places where there is false doctrine and false religion preached, and I do not want anyone to be in any doubt about why I am there. Also there are times when I am unable to speak to anyone, and passing motorists are able to see the witness of the cross. It is on days like that that I often feel the Lord reminding me of his words, 'You shall be my witness.'

Sometimes people come up to me and say, 'Why is your cross so small?' My reply is usually, 'Well it depends what you are comparing it to. If you compare it to what someone would wear around their neck, it is very big, but if you compare it to what our Lord died upon, it's rather small, but try carrying it for thirty kilometres and see how small it is!' My entire equipment, with water tanks fully loaded with water, Bibles, towels, chair, plus the cross and bowl, weighs in excess of 21kg (45lbs). After walking in blistering heat or sub-zero temperatures all day, one is fully aware that one has been carrying a load.

During the months in which God was preparing us as a family to go out, I faced every possible emotion that one could go through, as a father, as a husband, as a pastor and as an adult man—but knowing that first and foremost I was called to be a servant of the Lord. One of the fears I had to deal with was what people would think. Another was what would happen to my children, and once again God confirmed his call to me through his Scripture.

I have found David My servant; with My holy oil I have anointed him, with whom My hand will be established; My arm will also strengthen him. The enemy will not deceive him, nor the son of wickedness afflict him. But I shall crush his adversaries before him, and strike those who hate him. And My faithfulness, and My lovingkindness will be with him and in My name his horn will be exalted. I shall also set his hand on the sea, and his right hand on the rivers. He will cry to Me, 'Thou art my Father, my God, and the rock of my salvation' (Ps 89:20–26).

I had a deep sense that God was pouring his oil over me, assuring me of his protection, and that as he had called me, he would be faithful to give me favour; favour before man both in high places and low places, before the regenerate and the unregenerate, a door that would be open throughout the extremes of the body of Christ, favour in churches of every kind. In that same moment, I was crying out to God for the same assurance for my children and my family. God used that same beautiful psalm to assure me that his hand of blessing was on my children: 'My lovingkindness I will keep for him forever, and My covenant shall be confirmed to him. So I will establish his *descendants* forever, and his throne as the days of heaven' (Ps 89:28–29, italics mine).

The route I was to walk became another source of soul-searching—in prayer. One morning while praying, I was complaining to the Lord about the route I was to walk between Pretoria and Cape Town. I asked, 'Lord, how can you make me walk through the Karroo? It is so broad and so arid and there are very few towns or people.' The Karroo is an area of semi-desert, covered only by rock and a small tumbleweed type bush. It spans many hundreds of kilometres and the heat at certain times of the year is extreme during the day with temperatures plummeting below zero at night. I sensed the Lord saying, 'But that's not the route I want you to walk.' This set Carol and me praying over maps and atlases until the Lord carefully showed us our course. Instead of walking directly to Cape Town—a distance of some 1,500 kilometres—we were to start off in virtually the opposite direction, travelling the back routes of the Transvaal, through into Natal, down towards Durban, then on into the Transkei, following South Africa's coastline through the Ciskei and on round to Cape Town. By so directing us the Lord added at least 1,200 kilometres, more than the length of the journey. The route was set!

We decided that Carol and the children would travel with me by caravan and car, providing a back-up as I walked. They would follow me each day, or go ahead of me, as was most convenient for the family. At night I would be picked up by car, taken back to the caravan and then dropped off the next day at my previous stopping point. The children were to do their schoolwork in the caravan, and Carol would teach them. God's entire plan was becoming very clear. Yet even in all this, God was to reveal his hand by testing us and then showing his faithfulness. A few weeks before we were due to head out, I was speaking about evangelism to some of the young adults in our church one night. When I emerged from the meeting, I discovered that my small Japanese car was gone. It had been stolen. A few days later the police located it in Soweto. When I went to see it, it was like going to the mortuary to identify a dead body. It had been totally stripped and there was very little left of it.

During those days, I had found myself praying with a Jewish man, who had just given his life to Jesus. As he sat with his feet in the bowl, he said to me, 'Dave, pray that my children will come to know the Lord.' I explained the power of agreement from the word of God, sharing the verse, 'Again I say to you, that if two of you agree on earth about anything that they may ask, it shall be done for them by My Father who is in heaven' (Mt 18:19). We then prayed, 'agreeing' for his children's salvation. That evening I received the most excited phone call from the man saying that his children had just given their hearts to Jesus. He asked if he could bring them across and if I would mind working through with them what they had just done. A few days later he arrived with his children and once we had finished ministering to them, the man sat back in his chair. He said, 'Dave, I heard that your car got stolen. What are you doing about it?' I replied that I was sorry to sound so naive, but that I was doing the only thing I knew to do, and that was to trust the Lord, as I did not have any money to buy a new car.

He replied, 'But you are going off in two weeks across the nation. How are you going to pull your caravan?'

'I guess that Carol and the children will have to pull it by hand because God didn't say to us that we were to go if we had a car; he just told us that we were to go.' At that the man pulled out some registration papers from his pocket. He said, 'I have a car outside here that I have already had made roadworthy for you. If you don't like it, you can sell it and get what you like.'

'What kind of car is it?' I asked, wondering if it would pull a caravan.

'A Mercedes Benz,' he replied.

Hastily I responded, 'No, it's quite all right; we like that car.'

Finally, on the 2nd October 1988, after much planning and preparation, I stepped out onto the dusty streets of Soweto—and soon came face-to-face with my ultimate test of obedience: that rendezvous with seven gangsters in the dingy back-yard shed.

*   *   *

Time seemed momentarily frozen as my assailants pressed mockingly closer. An oppressive sense of evil pervaded the gloom. Everything seemed to be happening in slow motion.

'Yes, Jesus,' I heard myself say deep within, 'I am prepared to die now for you.'

In a flash, the Holy Spirit intervened, dropping into my consciousness a word of knowledge about the gangster directly in front of me. (For those unfamiliar with the term, a word of knowledge is supernatural knowledge imparted directly to one's mind by the Spirit of God.) Immediately I spoke the information to him, telling him about his life and what he had done. He was visibly taken aback. Then I had a word of knowledge about the next man, and the next and the next. The seven were thunderstruck by what I said to each of them. They instantly backed off, and over the next hour each of them, one after the other, sat with their feet in the bowl and surrendered their lives to Jesus. I ministered to them, bringing healing as they confessed and repented of what God had revealed in their lives. Suddenly there was a loud knocking on the door of the shed. One of the men unbolted it, and there stood a black man who, to this day, I am convinced was sent by the Lord.

'Excuse me, sir, are you all right?' he asked. 'I have been following you around for the last two days and watching you. I love Jesus.' After my reassuring him that I was indeed all right, he asked where I ate when I was on the road.

'Usually I don't eat. I just drink the water from my water tank.'

'Then you must come and eat at my house.' He led me through the narrow, dirty, dusty streets of the township, winding through one block then another, eventually arriving at a tiny home. He and his family promptly cooked me a lavish meal, a banquet fit for a king.

What a day! God had not only delivered me from death, but treated me to a banquet. As I finished off that evening the words of the apostle Paul were ringing through my mind: 'Thanks be to God, who gives us the victory through our Lord Jesus Christ' (1 Cor 15:57). Turning into bed that night I was deeply grateful to the Father for his faithfulness, for the blessing of his protective hand and for the honour of fulfilling the task to which he had called me.

The last day of my ten-day stint in Soweto dawned. As I was walking, witnessing about Jesus and occasionally washing feet, I rounded a corner and saw ahead of me a seething angry mob of about two hundred people. They ranged in age from eighteen to about twenty-two and were protesting about some grievance to do with the running of a college. I instantly feared for my safety, and turned for reassurance to the believers who were with me, only to see them running for their lives. I was about to join them when I sensed the Holy Spirit saying, 'The cross stands firm; it never retreats. Walk right into the middle of that crowd.' Gritting my teeth, I walked on into the middle of them. They closed around me and began jostling me but I was able to love them in Jesus and started handing out stickers and sharing the love of Jesus. Suddenly a calm came over the crowd and I was able to preach about the peace of God that passes all understanding. Praise God! I could not help thanking him for his protection.

Finally, late that evening just before I left Soweto, I was again reminded that God is not only an awesome God to be revered, but also the God who invented laughter. Indeed, Jesus came that our joy might be complete. About five of us were walking up a dusty hill, when a boisterous group of piccanins (small black children) burst out of some houses we were passing. With open-mouthed astonishment they gazed at the passing parade—the cross, bowl, chair, water tanks and other paraphernalia.

'Who are they?' said one.

'Dunno,' answered his equally puzzled friend.

'I know,' suddenly shrieked a third, 'They're the A-team.' We all rocked with laughter, feeling an easing of our burdens and fatigue as we were compared to their current TV heroes. Praise God for his love and goodness.

Ah, Soweto! Sometimes walking through its mass of humanity living in absolute poverty, one wonders if it isn't a little bit like shooting at Mount Everest with a peashooter. But I thank the Lord for allowing me the privilege of carrying his torch in a place like Soweto.

3
Standing in the Gap

Soweto with all its vivid memories was behind me, and it was now the official start of my walk through South Africa along the route God had shown us. At 2.30 pm on Sunday 16th October 1988, we arrived at the Union Buildings in Pretoria, South Africa's equivalent of America's White House. Much to my amazement a crowd of several hundred people had gathered. I was overwhelmed to say the least. Then the worship team from my home church led the singing of that powerful prophetic song:

> Shine, Jesus shine,
> Fill this land with the Father's glory,
> Blaze, Spirit, blaze,
> Set our hearts on fire.
> Flow, river flow,
> Flood the nations with grace and mercy,
> Send forth your word, Lord,
> And let there be light.

I then spoke for a short time, proclaiming hope for the nation and the potential of God in each person. After a time of prayer, we called representatives from all the churches present. There were Methodists, Baptists, a black lady from the Anglican church, people from independent churches, restoration churches and folk from the Diepkloof Community Church in Soweto, as well as many from my home church in Robinhills. There was also a young man representing the Afrikaans N G Kerk which thrilled me. After washing a number of people's feet we moved across with the crowd to have our photographs taken in front of the Union Buildings, and the big moment had arrived. I took my first symbolic steps of the long pilgrimage between Pretoria and Cape Town.

That night as I climbed into bed, I thanked God for his faithfulness and love. I knew his hand was upon me, yet as I pondered the awesomeness of the task ahead, I felt totally inadequate. All I could pray was, 'Please help me. I need your help.'

I spent the next two days in Pretoria, meeting and talking to many devout men of God; then I headed out of town, aware that God was once more showing me something new. As Christians, we live in 'comfort zones' we have built around ourselves. As I moved out on the road, I knew I was having to step out of my comfort zone, and sensed that God would continually take me out of my different comfort zones during the months ahead.

A lot happened during the next six months as I gradually worked my way towards the Natal town of Pietermaritzburg. My bodily fitness increased through carrying the cross and bowl plus heavy pack for hundreds of kilometres, and my spirit was encouraged daily by the 'divine appointments' set up by the Holy Spirit. I was also privileged to make a short trip overseas during this time, ministering in England and Iceland. Naively thinking at the outset that the entire trip would take little more than six months in total, I had covered less than a fifth of the distance by April the next year. However I was becoming content to let the Lord dictate my pace, and as I wound my way through the beautiful Valley of a Thousand Hills, between Pietermaritzburg and Durban, my heart sang. It was lovely just to be out on the road in autumn, passing by huge bluegums, walking round sharp curves, thrilling at the panoramic views of Natal's lush green landscape.

A car drew up beside me and its occupant enquired where I was headed. His expression as I told him I was walking to Cape Town—which is almost in the opposite direction—was a sight to behold. After I explained further, he offered me a lift which I declined. He then urged me to come home with him where he had a bicycle he would give me. I eventually explained that my wife had a perfectly good car, and if I wanted, I could get a lift with her—but then wouldn't meet lovely people like him.

Slogging up the next steep hill, I noticed an old pick-up truck toiling its way past me, heavily laden with several of the local rural people. Cresting the hill, I found the truck had stopped and its driver, a dear little man, was standing next to it waiting for me. Strongly resembling a hillbilly, he wore a huge battered straw hat and an old khaki shirt and shorts that looked about five sizes too big for him. Little did I realise as I approached him that I was about to undergo one of the most heart-rending experiences of my life.

Standing erect, with his hands on his hips, he introduced himself as Lieutenant-Commander John Whitehead (not his real name), saying he had been a submarine commander in the Royal Navy during the last war. I couldn't help wondering however if these titles had been self-imposed.

'I believe you are a man who prays,' he said, keeping his gaze fixed upon me. I later discovered that he had heard about me from a local resident who had seen me on a TV programme.

'You bet I do,' was my response, whereupon he informed me that his house had been robbed ten times in the last three months.

'Please would you come and pray over it for me?' was his plaintive request. So I jumped on the back of his little truck, squeezing in among the local rural African folk, and went bumping off over an unmade road.

His house—if one could call it that—was one of the most run-down, dilapidated shacks I have ever seen. The windows were covered with old planks, and rusty barbed wire zigzagged across the boards. The interior was filthy, and he informed me that over the years he had sold his furniture to stay alive. One room was piled high with an assortment of rusty scrap metal, rotting wood and nails that had obviously been lying around, rusting and deteriorating over the years. The house smelt dank and the walls were covered in damp green moss. Progressing down the dark passage, I noticed strange objects stuck on the doors. In answer to my enquiry, he told me that they were an African witch-doctor's charms placed there to prevent evil spirits from attacking him.

'That's a lie from the devil himself—you can't fight evil with evil,' I said, whereupon he armed himself with a hammer and chisel and struck the things from the doors.

Winding our way through horribly broken-down rooms, with furniture mostly of the packing-case variety, we ended up in a back room sitting on something that wasn't quite a bed and wasn't quite a couch. I held his hands and looked into his dear old face as he told me that he had no living relatives in the world. All he had to live on was a pension from the British Defence Force of £40 per month, with which he endeavoured to eke out an existence. My heart was overwhelmed with compassion for him and I truly saw him with the eyes of Jesus. With tears in my eyes I looked at him and asked, 'Mr Whitehead, has anyone ever told you about Jesus?'

'No,' he replied.

I thought to myself, eighty-one years old, a whole lifetime and more, and no one had ever bothered to tell this dear man the greatest news in the world. For the next half hour, I had the honour of telling him about the King of kings and the Lord of lords, the Jesus who came to seek and save the lost, who laid down his life for him. Mr Whitehead then sat with his feet in the bowl and surrendered his life to Jesus. I gave him a Bible, and he told me it was the first Bible he had ever had in his life. After this he introduced me to a young coloured girl, approximately seven years old, called Barbara. John explained that she was his granddaughter, as his daughter in England had been married to a West Indian before she had died and that he had taken her in to look after her. His only prayer was that God would spare him long enough to see her grown up. I couldn't help feeling that if the authorities found this young girl living in this situation, they would certainly remove her.

As we walked through the house we prayed for its cleansing from the powers of darkness, through the power of the Holy Spirit. I washed several people's feet, ministering to those in the house and praying with them for salvation before setting off once again. The next day I returned, bringing one of the local pastors to meet dear old John to see if their church would be open to following him up, praying for him and restoring his house, which would be a major project for any church. It is vital that we who are 'out in the field' work with the church. I believe that God has always worked through the church and that it is only as we bring this beautiful bride to perfection that God will work once again through her to usher in the return of her bridegroom Jesus.

People so often have the mistaken idea that to be out on the street doing evangelism, you have to be a 'spiritual blackbelt', that you have to walk along and whack around the ears everyone who crosses your path, and that if you don't come back with glowing reports of having at least ten converts within a two hour period you are some kind of dismal failure. It is the deep desire of my heart to prove exactly the converse of this. As I have mentioned before, there is no success or failure in the kingdom of God, only obedience. I find that when I am out on the street, the only thing the Holy Spirit requires is for me to be sensitive and to flow with him, and it never ceases to amaze me what God will do when we are simply available.

One day, as I was approaching the outskirts of greater Durban, accompanied by a dear pastor friend Gary Deetlefs, we were taking a midday siesta from the scorching, humid midday sun so typical of that area. While we were resting beneath a tree I noticed that we were outside a rather large conference centre. As we sat there I felt a strong nudge from the Holy Spirit to go in. Once the siesta was over, we proceeded to do just that.

As we made our way towards the reception area I noticed a large number of cars and realised that there must be a conference in session. We greeted the receptionist and asked what conference was taking place. She replied that it was the National Conference for one of the major trade unions in the country. The background to our trade unions is that they have often been used as a militant wing of hatred to break down the system of oppression that has held so many black people in bondage. These trade unions were also known to be very Marxist-orientated and this was prior to the collapse of the Iron Curtain.

My immediate reaction was, 'Praise the Lord! Do you think I would be able to address the trade union?' The receptionist got such a fright she nearly fell off her seat! You must remember that she had a man standing in front of her with a cross and bowl under his arm. She stammered, 'I am only the receptionist here; I have no control over what goes on in the conferences.' She did, however, go on to tell us that the conference was about to go into lunchtime recess and offered to introduce us to the trade union leader. This done, he informed us that they did not have long for lunch and suggested that we join him at his table for the meal. Within minutes we found ourselves seated at the table having lunch with the trade union leader. After lunch, Gary and I took the leader outside and shared the gospel with him plainly and clearly, before he continued with his pressurised programme. In fact, the rest of the meeting had gone back into session without him as we stood in the corridor and he prayed a prayer of commitment, receiving Jesus. I would like to believe that was the beginning of a softening of heart and a change of spirit within the life of that trade union with all its hostility.

Finally I was in Durban, chatting to the people on the streets, mingling with the crowds, and washing feet on

West Street, the main street of this holiday-makers' paradise. After the relative serenity of the open road, the pace of my life rapidly quickened with meetings, ministers' fraternals and the like. But in the midst of it all, I sensed the Lord saying, 'I want to speak to you as I have a word for this city.'

One of the things I have been learning from the very moment the Lord first started to call me to this rather unusual ministry is never to rush in but to be sure that it is God who is speaking. Often my ministry out on the road seems to provoke impulsive responses from people who arrive at my caravan or doorstep and announce brightly, 'Praise the Lord, Brother Dave; God has told me to walk with you.'

Usually I have never clapped eyes on the people before, and certainly God has not told me about them. Often the impression I get from them is that a spur of the moment decision is all it takes to embark on a calling of this nature. Usually I end up going to great lengths to explain that it wasn't simply that I had a vision from the Lord some enchanted evening and the next day stepped out with the cross and bowl, but that the calling-out took place over a fourteen-month period. Day by day, step by step, God confirmed and reconfirmed his word to me as I began to ease myself out of my normal pastoral function within the life of the church. Even then, God continually allowed me to walk through the fire, testing me, checking out my heart and integrity, making sure I didn't see myself as some lone ranger or maverick separate from the church. I go on to explain that I clearly see myself as part of the church, truly believing that the church will be the vehicle to usher in Christ's return, and that I am accountable and in submission to an eldership in the form of a council of brothers who believe in what God has called me to do. In short, decisions out on the road aren't to be taken lightly.

On this occasion, a dear friend of ours came down from Johannesburg with his family, and I sensed the Lord say, 'I have brought Ashton down to pray with

you, to confirm my word to you and to encourage you.'
Many times during my walk as I have entered South
African towns and cities, I have been aware of the Lord
giving me a strategy for that particular area. Often it is
a real spiritual battle to hear the word clearly, requiring
many hours of spiritual warfare and praying in the Spirit.
So I was grateful for Ashton's presence, and asked him
to join me in praying and waiting on the Lord.

Next morning we rose early and headed for Anstey's
Beach, where we had decided to pray and seek God's
will for the city. My fourteen-year-old daughter Carynne
expressed a desire to be a part of this, but said she would
stay in the caravan and intercede from there. At the
beach, Ashton and I split up; he walked south and I
walked up towards the north end. Placing my Bible on
a rock, I walked to the water's edge and stood there with
the wavelets lapping around my ankles.

'Lord, I know this could take many hours, but I also
know that your Holy Spirit could do a quick work,' I
murmured. Then taking my Bible, I began waiting on
God in earnest. Praise the Lord, he did do a quick work
and in little more than two hours I began to sense God
clearly showing me his plan for the city of Durban.

I was led to Genesis 18, where Abraham was pleading
with the Lord for the cities of Sodom and Gomorrah. He
said to God,

Wilt Thou indeed sweep away the righteous with the wicked?
Suppose there are fifty righteous men within the city; wilt
Thou indeed sweep it away and not spare the place for the
sake of the fifty righteous who are in it? (Gen 18:23–24).

So the LORD said, 'If I find in Sodom fifty righteous within
the city, then I will spare the whole place on their account'
(Gen 18:26).

I felt sure that God was calling me to rally fifty
righteous men in Durban to pray against the powers
of darkness surrounding the city. Durban is known
throughout South Africa and beyond its borders as a

holiday paradise, a city of glamour and glitter, but God showed me that this was just a thin veneer. Beneath the bright facade of this port city, I sensed, was great perversity, with prostitution, vice of all description and extensive drug abuse.

Specifically, I felt God telling me to rally the fifty righteous men—the fathers, the clergy, the pastors and ministers of the city—and to gather them before the war memorial in front of the city hall. We were then to march down West Street in the early evening and gather down at the sea-front with other Christians to plead for the city and to come against the powers of darkness that ruled and held the city captive. I sensed the Lord calling us to pray through the night and promising that as we prayed he would be faithful to break the devil's holds over the city.

Excitedly, I ran down the beach to meet Ashton, only to find him heading towards me. I could hardly contain what I felt God was saying, but bit my tongue and asked if God had said anything to him. His reply was that he had a passage of Scripture that he felt God was speaking but didn't understand it. He said, 'I have this here,'

Now may the God who gives perseverance and encouragement grant you to be of the same mind with one another, according to Christ Jesus; that with *one accord* you may with *one voice* glorify the God and Father of our Lord Jesus Christ (Rom 15:5–6, italics mine).

My heart leapt as he spoke; I knew this was God confirming what he had just told me about bringing the pastors, ministers, priests and clergy together: that he was calling them to come with one heart and one voice to be a testimony to the glory of Jesus. I thanked God that once again in his faithfulness, he was confirming his word.

I then shared with Ashton what God had revealed to me and he felt that it was right, but we prayed once again to make absolutely sure that this in fact was God's voice. While I was praying a wave of doubt came into

my mind. I asked, 'God, what happens if the fifty
righteous men won't come?' After all, I was hardly
known in this big city and what right had I to approach
not one, but fifty of the men of God? The Holy Spirit
swiftly cut in and reminded me of the place in the Bible
where Moses stood on his own before God and turned
God's heart to the whole nation of Israel. I was aware
of the Lord saying, 'I will provide the fifty righteous
men, but even if I choose not to, I want you to pray on
your own for the city of Durban.' One thing the Lord
has now shown me is that I need to be prepared to be
obedient on my own, even if other people are not
prepared to join me.

Once God had confirmed his word to us, Ashton and
I hurried back to the caravan where we gathered our
families together. When I asked them to turn to Genesis
18, Ashton's wife, Grace, let out a scream. She said that
Carynne had been praying at the same time as Ashton
and myself and that was the exact scripture that God
had led Carynne to—a relatively obscure passage hidden
among more than a thousand chapters in the Bible.
We rejoiced and thanked God for his faithfulness in
confirming his word step by step, moment by moment.

The next days were taken up with making a small start
on what God had shown me to do, contacting pastors,
ministers and priests of every persuasion within the
body of Christ. God started to show me at this time why
I had been involved in so many pastors' fraternals and
groupings over the previous week. Even though I had
often felt frustrated, it had been his will, because he was
already laying the foundation for what lay ahead.

One of the first people I was able to talk to about what
God had said, was a man called Mike Eltringham. Mike,
in addition to being the pastor of The Lord's Place, is
the Durban co-ordinator for the International Fellowship
of Christian Churches. He praised the Lord for what I
shared with him and said that for a long time, he had
been praying that a city eldership would be raised up.
He undertook to rally as many men as possible for the

march that God had laid on our hearts and for the night
of intercession. He assured me that I would not have to
stand praying alone, but that there would be at least two
of us on the given night. The days that followed
continued to be hectic, phoning and rushing around to
the authorities to gain permission, under the prevailing
state of emergency, to hold our march as well as our
night of prayer on the sea-front.

Christian marches have subsequently become commonplace in South Africa, but at that time anyone who
desired to hold a march of any description was suspected
of being subversive or Marxist. Application had to be
made through the law courts as well as through the
Commissioner of Police. In addition, Durban has a city
police force of which they are very proud, and which I
am told is the oldest police force still functioning within
the history of South Africa. They too had to give their
blessing to the event. This, coupled with the fact that
the authorities had demanded that I take out a public
liability insurance to protect all those marching, along
with trying to co-ordinate fifty very busy men from
diverse backgrounds within the body of Christ, was a
fairly harassing experience, to say the least. But, praise
the Lord, by lunchtime on the Thursday before the
designated Friday night we had fifty godly righteous
men who had all agreed to be part of the march and the
night of prayer for the city of Durban.

Friday dawned, and from the first I knew that we had
a battle on our hands. It was a cold, miserable, windy
day, the most adverse weather we had had down at the
coast for a month. The wind kept coming up exceptionally strongly, the clouds were black and getting darker,
yet we felt throughout the day that there was about to
be a spiritual breakthrough. At five o'clock that evening
it was the blackest it had been all day, and as we gathered
in front of the city hall waiting for the pastors to appear
we felt that maybe this would be the real test of who
the 'righteous men' really were. By 5.30 however there
were more than the fifty righteous men gathered in front

of the war memorial outside the city hall in Gardiner Street. With a sense of amazement, I noted the prophetic inscription on the war memorial: 'Tell this to the next generation: "Unless the seed fall to the ground and die, it cannot bear fruit"'! We were the next generation, forty years on from the Second World War. So as the march began in the gathering gloom, the fathers of the city called out in turn to the next generation that which the fathers of the previous generation had written.

Thus glorifying God, and with the musicians in front of us, we headed into West Street and down towards the sea-front, with much fanfare and banner-waving. It was glorious to see this testimony to the city of Durban. As we arrived at the sea-front there were several hundred present, and we began to praise and worship the Lord and intercede. At times the crowd would lay prostrate before the Lord on the rough brick paving of the kind of amphitheatre which formed the major access to South Africa's main and busiest sea-front. Each hour was led by a different church grouping or church leader. There were Anglicans, Methodists, Nazarenes, Presbyterians, Restoration-type churches, Faith churches, IFCC and The Durban Christian Centre. Each took a turn. At the end of each hour, I would wash the feet of the leaders of that church that had been leading, as well as of others who came to salvation or needed ministry. In spite of persistent rain, the faithful Christian people of Durban continued to come and go throughout the night and the fifty righteous men stood firm, waiting for the dawn to appear.

We felt sure that the enemy's hold over the city was bound and that as we had cried out to God, taking authority by the power of the Holy Spirit, the prevailing powers had been broken. We stood in awe as we felt that perhaps 'the church at Durban' was being born. Between 3 and 4 am we started prophesying life back into the city. We started to see it as God wished it to be. What was born as an infant would surely come to the full maturity of adulthood. Ian Goulay, a pastor friend of mine from Amanzimtoti, told of a vision that God had given him that night as he saw the fifty righteous men marching down West Street, a vision of West Street clogged with Christians marching, even as it appears when 12,000 runners stand bobbing up and down at the annual Comrades' Marathon Event, and other Christians thronging the pavements cheering them on as they marched down to the sea-front.

At 6 am as the sun was rising, we finished with a time of celebration, all departing with hearts overflowing with gratitude for what God had done and that the power of his Spirit had broken. We praised God for what he had brought to birth. 'Thank you, Lord: what you brought to birth through prayer, we saw in reality ten days later. Glory to your name, Lord; continue to be glorified; thank you for the privilege of prayer.' The anointing and favour of God seemed to abound, and it was truly like walking with Jesus as I headed south out of Durban and started to weave my way through the little villages dotted along the magnificent Natal South Coast.

I was walking one evening through the small town of Amanzimtoti, accompanied by my son, Ronnie-Russ, who was carrying the cross and bowl. It was already dark and we were waiting for Carol to arrive with the car to fetch us, when suddenly a car drew up alongside us. A very refined-looking lady emerged and as I looked closely at her I could see that she was weeping. She said, 'Dave, I have been looking everywhere for you. I heard you were in the area.' Just then Carol drew up and I called her to join us. The lady said to me, 'Look at my face; I know what it is like to be unclean.' As I looked, I could see that the left-hand side of her face was covered with marks which she explained were a form of herpes. As she wept, she explained that she had been to several of the country's top skin specialists and that they could do nothing for her. We sat her down just off the main road, and as she sat weeping with her feet in the bowl, the Lord said to me, 'David, wash her face.' The words of Peter ran through my mind, 'Not only my feet, but my head and my hands also, Lord.' The Lord then gave me a word of knowledge which I spoke to her and said that the Lord wanted to wash her inside out and that he was going to cleanse her and set her free from things that had held her captive.

As I washed her face, I felt certain, as the water mingled with her tears, that God was healing her. God further told me to tell her that each morning she was to wash her face with clean water and to thank God for her healing. The next Sunday morning, I preached at a celebration in the Amanzimtoti Civic Centre, a large impressive building. At the end of the meeting I saw a lady running through the crowd, her face beaming like an angel; truly the glory of the Lord was upon her. It was the same lady whose face I had washed, and she exclaimed joyfully, 'Look, Dave, there's not a mark on my face. Glory to Jesus.'

The glory of the Lord just seemed to continue as I approached the small town of Warner Beach, where I was to have some of my most significant experiences with the cross and bowl. I was accompanied by a pastor friend, Terry Fouche, from Durban. As Terry and I headed towards Warner Beach, we had a very real sense of the presence of Jesus with us. At one stage a lady stopped her light delivery vehicle, jumped out and asked if she could give each of us a kiss. She hugged us and wept as we washed her feet and encouraged her in Jesus. We moved along the road, praying and praising and worshipping God, chatting to one or two people, wondering at the awesomeness of putting a sticker on a little child and wondering what impact the transference of spirit would have upon his family.

As we came into Warner Beach, we had the most amazing experience. On almost every corner, people were waiting for us. Having heard that I was coming, they were waiting to be prayed with, coming to be saved, coming to be ministered to. As we were washing feet and prophesying over a group of women, another woman pulled up in her car and we were able to pray for her healing and set her free from hurts in her life. Further along the pavement we ministered to an elderly couple, who asked to be healed in Jesus' name, then washed another woman's feet. There were white women, black women, white men, people of every description, and it was beautiful just to meet the needs in their lives, to wash their feet and to show the servant-love of Jesus. We saw several born again, and it was a joy to move along in the presence of Jesus, in between meeting people waiting for us on almost every street corner.

At midday, we encountered a woman who was truly saddened about the state of her step-son. The burden of grief she was carrying was very evident to Terry and myself as she wept and explained that he was angry; angry with the world, angry with his family, and angry with God. At the age of nineteen, he had already been up on two counts of attempted murder. I sensed almost a desperation in the mother's heart. Once again we explained the power of 'agreement' and we agreed for that young man's salvation and that the Holy Spirit would lure him by the power of God.

Towards the end of the day, as we were leaving the outskirts of Warner Beach, we were once again greeted by a small group of people. As I was chatting to them, I saw out of the corner of my eye, a young man standing a small distance away. I called him across. He couldn't even look me in the eye and suddenly I felt the power of God come upon me as I challenged him about his hardness of heart. I said to him, 'You have been running away from God.'

'Yes.'

'You don't want to keep running.'

'No.'

'Jesus is calling you to repent,' I said.

'I know,' he responded.

I said, 'Sit down and take your shoes off,' which he promptly did, placing his feet in the bowl as he surrendered his life to Jesus. There wasn't much eloquence about my speech or confrontation, but his heart had melted as Jesus touched him.

Unbeknown to me, this was the same young man whose mother had stood in agreement with us at lunchtime that day. As I was washing his feet, an aunt of his had come walking along the road. She ran away weeping with joy, saying that she could not believe what she was seeing as this young man sat with his feet in the bowl and encountered Jesus, asking for forgiveness and surrendering his sin at the foot of the cross.

Warner Beach was a place that I will never forget. I shall always remember how people waited on the streets as they heard that the man with the cross and the bowl was coming, how they loved us, how they showered us with their blessing, how they were so open to Jesus, and to embracing what Jesus wanted to do. That night my prayer was simply, 'Thank you, Father God, for seeing your hand move in such an unprecedented way today. Thank you for the privilege of allowing me to carry this bowl. Thank you, Lord, for the privilege of carrying this cross. Thank you, Father, for what you are doing in my life. Thank you for the way that you are moulding me and teaching me dependence on you. Keep me at the foot of your cross, Lord. Amen.'

4
Putting Your Hand to the Plough

Sometimes, listening to Christians talk about their blessings, one can get the impression that the Christian walk is all plain sailing with no problems, a continual bed of roses without any thorns. As any mature Christian will tell you, that is simply not true. Yes, it is a life beyond compare; yes, there are the blessings and the hallelujahs. But there is another side to it too. Jesus was the most successful, victorious man this world has ever seen, yet his most triumphant moment on earth came in death. The Christian walk is just what it says—a walk. And Jesus is concerned not so much with how we begin as how we continue to the end. He clearly illustrated this in the parable of the talents, where all three of the men concerned had the same start and were honoured to have been chosen as custodians of their master's fortune. We see the heart of Jesus clearly as he comes to the point of the parable where the master returns to settle accounts. Only those who had been faithful and finished well and borne good fruit won the master's commendation: 'Well done, thou good and faithful servant.'

I believe that far more than any wildly enthusiastic beginning with a rush of good resolutions, the Lord is interested in entering into an ever-deepening, enduring long-term relationship with us. I believe the way this is done, as I have the understanding of Scripture, is that God is constantly seeking to refine us. His modus operandi is the sifting business.

Consider Joseph. The child Joseph had a dream of

binding sheaves with his brothers in the field, and his sheaf had risen up and stood erect. His brothers' sheaves then bowed down to his sheaf. As Joseph interpreted this prophetic dream to his brothers, jealousy rose in their hearts and they began to plot against him. The result was that this man, who was being prepared by God to rule, was thrown into a well and eventually sold into slavery.

Then, as he rose to a position of seniority in Potiphar's house, not only did he have the temptation placed before him by Potiphar's wife, but as he resisted he was framed for adultery, and slung into prison. As if that was not enough, as he began to interpret dreams in prison, his sifting process intensified as he lay there forgotten. Finally, years later, he was freed, the sifting process complete, as God had now prepared him for a position of leadership where he would be able to rule under the power of the Holy Spirit.

There are parallels in the life of Jesus. As with Joseph, the sifting began in his childhood as he was about his Father's business, teaching in the temple. He found himself being scolded by his parents, who, seemingly, for the moment did not understand the anointing and calling on young Jesus. Then, just as he seemed to be having a reprieve as he went through baptism by John in the Jordan, he found himself thrust into the wilderness to be tempted by the devil for forty days and forty nights. He went on to face every temptation that we could ever face. The devil dangled suicide and wealth, fame and power before him, and as God allowed his own beloved Son to be sifted, the relationship between them developed, in preparation for the moment when Jesus would be released to rule in the power of his Father.

The exciting revelation for us as Christians is that 'if the Spirit of Him who raised Jesus from the dead dwells in you, He who raised Christ Jesus from the dead will also give life to your mortal bodies through His Spirit, who indwells you' (Rom 8:11). Paul goes on to say, 'If children, heirs also, heirs of God and fellow heirs with

Christ, if indeed we suffer with Him, in order that we may also be glorified with Him' (Rom 8:17). The logical conclusion of all this is that if we are joint heirs with Jesus and are to enjoy his full inheritance with all its benefits, if his Spirit dwells in us, then we too must be sifted with him, so that God can operate through us as pure vessels that are glorifying to him.

You may ask, what about the new believer who performs signs and wonders and has not yet been sifted? Well, I believe that God is an encourager. It's like the little boy who was given a hen as a gift and stood for hours peering longingly through the fence of the chicken run, waiting expectantly for the hen to lay her first egg. Eventually that evening he returned to the kitchen with his trophy high in the air, exclaiming with pride how wonderful it was to be the owner of a hen that could lay such a marvellous egg. What he didn't realise was that when he was not looking, his father had removed an egg from the fridge and placed it beneath the hen. I believe there are times in all our lives when God in his faithfulness 'puts an egg under the hen' on our behalf, simply to bless us and to glorify his name. In the long term, however, God requires a deep enduring relationship with each of us.

As I live my life, I see that God continues to sift me as he teaches me to endure in two totally different dimensions. The first deals with the spiritual. It starts with my prayer life as he assists me to pray with fervour, from the heart, not mindlessly and not repetitively. Then in the area of Bible reading he consistently challenges me about how often we do not even remember what we have read, let alone act on it. Perpetually, too, he convicts me of slander, whether 'justified' or not. So often Christians are tempted to imply or insinuate things against their brothers and sisters and in so doing break the heart of God. Another area of righteousness where God continues to deal with me is in bringing me to the place where I can see others exalted beyond me, and not be sucked into the pit of jealousy and pride which so often dogs people in ministry. God wants to touch each of us in our lives in these areas, not as a one-off experience, but as a daily enduring and endearing relationship with him.

The second dimension in which God continues to sift me and cause me to endure, is far more practical, and yet often is the test of whether having put my hand to the plough, I am going to look back or not. For Jesus said, 'No one, after putting his hand to the plough and looking back is fit for the kingdom of God.' This area has to do with sheer physical endurance, and the overcoming of trials. Bear in mind that although I am able to walk in the victory of all the fulness that God would bless me with, nevertheless, he perpetually keeps his eye upon me and continually checks me out.

As I mentioned earlier, it took fourteen months from the time that God first started to speak to me before we were able to begin this 3,000 kilometre pilgrimage with the cross and bowl. We were all set and ready to go; then came the amazing blow of having our motor car stolen. Next, right in the starting blocks, knockout punch number two was delivered. Carol and I had returned home late one evening. I was leaning against one of the kitchen cupboards, chatting to Carol as she was making coffee, when suddenly she turned sharply to get something out of the refrigerator and her knee jumped clean out of joint. She rolled around writhing on the ground, and there was little I could do to comfort her as I desperately prayed in tongues over her. She was unable to move but just lay there crying on the floor as I rushed for a pillow to place under her head. When finally the pain began to subside, I hoisted her arm around my neck, and gently pulling her up, hobbled towards the bedroom with her.

The next day, the knee was still so weak that she could not walk on it. She attempted to limp around but the pain was excruciating. As the next few days ticked by, her knee seemed to get no better, but in fact seemed to be deteriorating and we decided that she would probably need major surgery. What were we to do? No motor car to pull our caravan, a wife needing major surgery, and every cent we had required for the major mission that lay before us. Were we to delay our departure? Was I to try and earn some extra money to purchase the new car and to finance Carol's operation? Then came the realisation: God didn't say, 'If you have a car and perfect health, you are to do that for which I called you,' he simply said, 'Do it.'

The miracle of the provision of the car then took place, and we decided that we would totally trust God to heal Carol by his mighty hand and continue in faithful obedience to what God had shown us. Daily we claimed God's healing for Carol's knee, and rapidly it began to improve. We realised that once again God was checking us out, sifting us to ensure we would be faithful stewards, able to be trusted with the fulness of the power of his Holy Spirit.

Persecution, criticism, mocking and misunderstanding are all part of the daily routine of road life. And while I can handle it and understand that it will come because Jesus warned us about it, I can't say that I ever fully get used to it or vaguely enjoy it. One learns to take it, however, and put up with it from the world. One thing though that I have never got used to, and find one of the most painful aspects of my entire call, is when the attack comes from within the body of Christ, the very place that one least expects it. I do thank God for the favour that he has given me among his church and how 90% of the time across the full spectrum of his body the church runs out with arms extended exclaiming, 'Blessed is he who comes in the name of the Lord.' Yet sometimes the stones come from the enemy as he manages to get in and cause God's people to throw them.

One such occasion almost finished me. It began on a damp morning as I was heading through a beautiful scenic area not far from a little country village. The contrasts that hit me that day later seemed almost impossible to comprehend as stemming from the same root. As my feet pounded along the side of the road, I could hear the cross creaking against the straps that supported my water tanks. I noticed a kombi (minibus) drive past me when all of a sudden it braked to a halt in the middle of the road. The driver's door flew open and a man jumped out, running a hundred metres or more to greet me. As he got to me, he flung his arms around me and thrust a Coke into my hand, rejoicing with me at the roadside as I shared with him some of the blessings that God had showered on me as I had been able to show the servant love of Jesus along the highways and byways. He told me that he was a Baptist pastor and excitedly scribbled his name and address on a piece of paper, asking me to come and preach in his church when I reached his town. As I watched him and his wife drive off into the distance I continued, completely overwhelmed and blessed by the expression of love that God had just allowed me to experience.

Some time later, as I trudged breathlessly up an incredibly steep hill, having just walked through a deluge of rain and been soaked to the bone, a motor car once again pulled over. The occupants of the car, a man and his wife, introduced themselves enthusiastically. The man was an Anglican priest from a nearby city and invited me to bring my family to stay at his home when we reached there. I thanked him and we chatted and shared about the goodness of God before linking hands at the roadside, praying together and bidding one another farewell. I continued joyously on my way along the edge of the beautiful forest fringing the road.

Suddenly to my delight I came upon a Christian conference centre. The grounds were very well kept and there seemed to be homes on the property belonging to the staff. With joy welling up inside my heart, I felt a deep sense of gratitude for faithful servants of Jesus, and decided to go in and bring them the greeting of the Lord. I made my way towards the house of the man in charge when suddenly I was confronted by two men. Without finding out who I was, or what I was really doing, or enquiring about how God had called me, these two men, born-again Spirit-filled believers, I am embarrassed to say, discharged an avalanche of spiritual abuse at me, the like of which I have never before had the misfortune of encountering. Minute after minute, for what seemed an eternity, they continued to abuse me, attempting to justify their actions and attitudes through the word of God. Aggressively they condemned me for being out on the road, 'doing my own thing', not being under the covering of a church. I was caught totally off-guard by this sudden attack from such an unexpected quarter.

I felt so utterly shaken, I was crying inside. Feebly, I attempted to explain to them that I was one who was sent, that I was accountable to a local church and eldership, that I did not see myself as separate from the church, but rather a part of the church. They seemed not to hear a single word I said, but continued with their verbal bombardment. Eventually, after some twenty minutes, they looked at one another with a gleeful expression and asked, 'Well, what can we do for you?', the first time in the entire period that it occurred to them to enquire the purpose of my visit. As I tried to explain, one looked at the other and then sniggered, 'Ha, ha, I suppose he wants to wash our feet.' I tearfully looked at them and said, 'I came to bring you greetings in the name of Jesus, but unfortunately because of your attitude I am compelled to retract them according to the word of God.'

Heartbroken, I turned and headed towards the gate which led to the main road. As I stood there, I did something I had never done before, and have never had to do since. I stood on the tarmac and shook the dust from my feet in accordance with what Jesus told his disciples to do in Luke 9:5, when people did not receive them. Then in a daze I moved on down the road heading to the beautiful small village at the foot of the hill. As I walked into the tiny village, my emotions were in turmoil. I couldn't think straight and it was difficult to

know even where I really was. Certainly the beauty of
the lovely little village never even penetrated as I literally
staggered into a shop. To this day I cannot remember
what I said to the lady behind the counter, but I do
remember ending up in a back room washing her feet.
How that happened could only be by the grace of God,
for indeed he is El Shaddai, the God who is more than
enough.

When I was born again, on the day that Jesus came
into my life, the Lord baptised me with his joy, and I
can truthfully say that it has never left me in all the years
that I have now walked with him. However, this time
it just seemed as if, like a bird with a broken wing, my
spirit had been broken. For two or three days my spirit
refused to lift. 'Why?' I asked God. 'Why could men
who seemingly were filled with the Spirit, have placed
themselves back under such bondage in their so-called
new-found freedom?' Why would Christians attack one
another? Or was I totally wrong in what I was doing?
Even though I had seen God's hand move so many times,
had he really called me to this?

Question after question came pounding through my
mind and spirit, which refused to lift. I had always
preached that part of the purpose of God's anointing
was to sustain us, and that the only way that we can
remain under God's anointing is to dwell in his presence
and abide in his word. As I was desperately attempting
to apply these principles to my life, God began to
minister to me. The Lord asked a question about a
promise that he had given to me long before I ever started
out on the road. He asked, in the words of Psalm 89:20–
21, 'Have I not found David My servant? With My holy
oil I have anointed him, with whom My hand will be
established; My arm also will strengthen him.'

I replied, 'Yes, Lord, you have.'

He went on to ask me another question: 'What about
Mark 16:15 where it says, "Go into all the world and
preach the Gospel to all creation"—are you doing that?'

I replied, 'Yes, Lord.' And I sensed the Holy Spirit

saying, 'My son, I am well pleased with you.' Then came the next verse, which was the Lord's parting words, 'You shall be My witnesses both in Jerusalem and in all Judea, Samaria, and even to the remotest part of the earth.' I began to understand that Jerusalem, in my case, was Johannesburg where our home church was; Judea in essence was the broader Transvaal, the province (state) which I had come from, and Samaria represented Southern Africa and the nations of the earth. Once again I sensed the Lord asking, 'Are you doing that?'

I replied, 'Yes, Lord,' but promptly raised an objection. 'What about the local church, Lord? Have I done wrong in being sent out?' And then as if a bolt of lightning hit me, the Lord clearly showed me a picture of Philip and the eunuch and he asked the question, 'Do you think that the eunuch would have come to know me and been baptised if Philip had remained in the local church? Did not I myself tell you to go?'

I responded, 'Yes, Lord,' and felt my spirit begin to rise.

Finally there came the beautiful restorative 'washing of the word' as he brought this verse to my mind:

My grace is sufficient for you, for power is perfected in weakness. Most gladly, therefore, I will rather boast about my weaknesses that the power of Christ may dwell in me. Therefore I am well content with weaknesses, with insults, with distresses, with persecutions, with difficulties, for Christ's sake; for when I am weak, then I am strong (2 Cor 12:9–10).

Suddenly I felt something break in the Spirit. I was free. God's anointing had once again broken the shackles that had tried to crush me. I knew that God had sustained me, that I was once again able to put my hand to the plough and not look back. Hallelujah!

Often people come up to me and ask me how I feel about what God has called me to do. With a deep sense of privilege I usually reply that I feel honoured that, when God's eye roamed to and fro throughout some

thirty million people in Southern Africa, seeking someone to be his servant and to show his servant-love by
washing feet, he chose me. However, part of the inner
challenge I face is that so often as I go into churches, in
order to encourage the body of Christ, I tend to speak
about the excitement and the high moments of what God
does out on the road. This can cause people to think
that I walk one long glory trail. The truth is that it is
90% slog and 10% glory, and it is only by the sustaining
grace of the Holy Spirit that we can ever begin to do
what God has called us to. Some days we seem to glide
on eagles' wings; other days it is sheer endurance, simply
pressing on step by step.

One such day occurred not long after Carol had
dropped me out in the country. It was a beautiful
summer's day and I hadn't been going for much more
than twenty minutes when suddenly the weather began
to change dramatically. The sky darkened ominously,
the heavens opened, lightning and thunder began to
crack and rumble all about me, and I could rapidly feel
myself becoming drenched to the skin. As the gravel on
the shoulder of the road became increasingly wet, it
worked its way into my right shoe, and I would have to
stop and empty it out about every 300 metres. Eventually
there was no point in continuing to do this as my socks
became totally saturated with mud. The rain continued
to pelt down and I could feel blisters forming underneath
my feet from the gravel that my shoe was shipping.
There was absolutely no shelter from the pouring rain
so I just had to keep going, knowing that if I stopped I
would suffer from exposure.

Eventually, the mud on the side of the road became
so slippery that it was like trying to walk on ice. I would
repeatedly slither and fall, then get up again, just forcing
myself to keep going. The road was narrow and heavy
with traffic, so there was no way that I could walk on
the tarred surface. Walking was almost impossible, yet
I couldn't stand still, so I just had to keep gritting my
teeth, crying out to the Lord and pressing on.

One thing I learned very early on in my walk is that people don't stand out in the pouring rain waiting to be witnessed to, so there was not even anyone to share the gospel with. As the day wore on, I became bitterly cold, and my body began to seize up. I was clad only in what my family affectionately calls my 'road uniform': a T-shirt that proclaims 'Jesus-washed feet . . . are happy feet', and shorts. I continued to press on, limping, my feet aching, slipping, sliding, desperately wanting to sit down, chilled to the marrow. Even in this sopping wet state I could feel the hot tears welling in my eyes. Eventually I cried out to God and said, 'God, what is this all about? Why am I out here? What am I doing here? Am I crazy?' Then came the still small voice of the Spirit as I sensed the Lord saying, 'No, David, I am just teaching you to endure; I am just checking you out.'

Finally after some six hours Carol arrived to collect me, and as my son began to load my water tanks, Bible, cross, bowl and other gear into the boot, I could hardly bend down to get into the car. I looked at Carol and said to her, 'If I were a quitter, today would be the day I quit,' but as Carol turned the car about and we headed back to base, I knew once again the Lord was saying, 'No one, after putting his hand to the plough and looking back, is fit for the kingdom of God.'

5
Mud Huts and Palaces

It was the middle of winter as we moved out from the small town of Kokstad in the south-east of Natal. The weather was freezing with temperatures as low as −6°, and our caravan offered little protection against these extremes of cold. Ahead of us lay the Transkei, not just another border, but an entirely different lifestyle for us as a family. South Africa is very much a mixture of the First and Third Worlds. It has been said that South Africa is a microcosm of the entire world with similar percentages of global haves and have-nots. Whether that is true or not, I do not know, but the fact remains that South Africa embraces wide extremes of living standards. The Transkei is unquestionably Third World, similar to much of the rest of rural Africa. Pronounced an 'independent homeland' under the apartheid system, it was the flagship of many such 'independent' countries subsequently created within the borders of South Africa.

After gaining independence, Transkei had as its first Prime Minister Paramount Chief Kaiser Matanzima. Although considered somewhat arrogant, he was reasonably straight in most of his dealings. After several years, he was succeeded by his brother George, who was later removed from office when a large fraud scandal was uncovered. George Matanzima was, in turn, replaced by Transkei's first woman Prime Minister, Stella Sigcau. Tragically, too, during her reign there were rumours of much corruption. In December 1987, she was removed from power by a bloodless coup, conducted by Major

General Bantu Holomisa, who with his military council took over the country. A quiet, unassuming but powerful leader, General Holomisa immediately began stamping out corruption with unwavering determination. In the military council's wisdom, while they removed Stella Sigcau as Prime Minister, they kept intact the entire cabinet under the leadership of its President Ndamase, so they legislated via a form of coalition between the cabinet and the military council.

Such was the background of the country we were about to enter. Ironically, although the Transkei posed such a challenge to us as a family in terms of environment, it was actually the land of my birth. In 1947 when I was born, my father had been the Methodist minister in the tiny village of Cala on the Transkei's north-western border, and I looked forward to tracing my roots back to the mission hospital where I was born.

A country of rolling hills, dotted with kraals and mud huts as far as the eye can see, the Transkei is a poor nation by any standards. Many of the people are still entrenched in a primitive lifestyle, embodying deep tribal traditions of ancestral spirit-worship. Poverty is compounded by the migrant labour system whereby many of the menfolk go to the larger cities of Southern Africa or to the mines to seek work.

The weeks preceding our entry into the Transkei saw much frenzied activity about the caravan, as we sought to make ourselves totally self-contained. We knew that the route which I was to walk through the country had almost no caravan parks or ablution facilities readily available. We first ensured that the caravan could supply its own electricity via a tiny generator. We then built water tanks into the caravan with the able help of Carol's brother, Ron, to ensure fresh water when we needed it. We even installed a hot water system, heated by gas, so that we could at least have a skimpy shower from time to time. This shower was to cause a high moment of humour at my expense during our preparations, much to Carrie and Ronnie's delight.

A few days before we left Kokstad, I decided that we would have a trial run to determine just how self-contained we actually were. I duly instructed the family that the next day we were not to use any of the outside facilities available to us. We would use the chemical toilets, we would wash all dishes and also do all our showering in the caravan. There were to be no exceptions whatsoever.

After being out on the road all that day, I needed to wash quickly before rushing off to address a ladies' meeting. I jumped into the portable shower, got myself wet, soaped myself all over—and then disaster struck. The shower dried up completely.

In my most composed 'fruits of the Spirit voice', I asked my children just who was playing the fool with the shower. The only answer was giggling from outside, and then it suddenly struck me, as I stood with shampoo in my hair, dripping with soap from head to toe, that I had forgotten to fill completely the water tanks under the caravan. My kind sympathetic children rolled around holding their sides as Dad sheepishly emerged, wiped the soap off himself with a towel and headed off fragrantly if somewhat stickily towards the ladies' meeting.

And so it was that, duly prepared, we left our First World environs and entered the Transkei.

It was a long, hot walk up Brooke's Nek and I was aware of snakes in the green grass as I climbed the steep hill. The hill seemed to go on and on, but it was lovely just being out on the road and greeting the many minibuses and other rural-looking vehicles flowing towards Kokstad from the Transkei. As I came over the crest of the very steep pass, I gazed down, saw the huts of the Transkei below and truly understood that I was in a different land. Immediately I was aware of goats, sheep, cattle and dogs roaming freely, often ambling across the main road unmindful of the traffic. Piccanins would scamper alongside me, happily propelling old bicycle wheels with sticks.

My first encounter with the Third World was a rather stunning situation. As I proceeded down the far side of Brooke's Nek, a bull in front of me suddenly took fright and darted over the road, right into the path of a speeding pick-up truck. As the truck crashed into him, the bull hurtled into the air and came back down onto the bonnet of the pick-up. The man jumped straight out of his damaged vehicle, pulled out a revolver and shot the injured beast dead. You can imagine the surprise on my face as all this happened in an instant right in front of me. I was grateful the man didn't turn round with his pistol and take the next shot at me, as I walked across to ask him if he was all right. I said, 'God bless you, sir,' but either he didn't hear me or was too stunned to respond, wordlessly picking up the pieces of his damaged vehicle before driving off into the distance.

I walked on deeper into the Transkei. Later that day I was joined by two little boys, pushing along—in typical rural fashion—home-made wire cars. Each wanted me to have a turn pushing his car, as they carried the cross and bowl with much enthusiasm and difficulty. I put stickers on them and gave them a hug and they journeyed with me for many, many kilometres, greatly delighted at being able to walk with me. I realised just how hungry children must be in this place when one of them found a rotting chicken head that had virtually decomposed and with much delight picked it up and began to eat it, eyes and all, just as a western child would eat an ice cream. We said our farewells and a little further on that evening Carol picked me up and I thanked God for being with me as I had journeyed into the Transkei that day. I thanked the Lord that night for what lay ahead and for what he was doing in our lives as a family. In this rural situation we had a deep sense that God was also preparing us for other parts of Africa.

We had attempted time and time again to secure a Xhosa interpreter before entering the Transkei (Xhosa being the language spoken in the Transkei); however all our writing, contacting and phoning various people had been to no avail. One thing we had learnt by this stage, however, is that where God calls and appoints, he always provides, and Jesus said, 'If you ask Me anything in My Name, I will do it' (Jn 14:14). One morning after I had been in the Transkei a few days, I was once again to experience the faithful hand of God meeting our needs. I had been walking for an hour or so when I passed a small village on the left-hand side of the road. Just beyond that there was a taxi pick-up and drop-off point, where many of the local Africans were selling their wares, including goats and chickens. I was standing trying to converse with the rural people at the roadside, those waiting to catch taxis and those buying and selling goods, and much to my frustration, not one of them could understand my English. Just then, two rather shady-looking white men pulled up in a car and asked me what I was doing. I started to share the gospel and the love of Jesus with them, whereupon one of them committed his life to the Lord. As he sat at the roadside and I washed his feet, the black rural onlookers erupted in jubilation, fully understanding what I was doing. After that, many of them queued to have their feet washed and for me to pray with them. To my delight I discovered that the motorist who had become a Christian spoke perfect Xhosa. He was able to interpret as I shared the gospel with the crowd, and I thanked God for sending someone in his perfect timing.

The people of the Transkei were so open and friendly that often I could not help feeling that their openness to the gospel had almost a naivete about it. One afternoon as I was journeying through the hilly country, I started chatting to some students who were going back to their local school. As we walked the kilometres together, more and more joined in, until eventually there were several hundred of them, many of whom could speak good English. As we were approaching their school they realised they were late, but one young man pleaded with me to wash his feet. As I did so, a crowd gathered around most excitedly as they sensed the Spirit of God fall at that moment. By this stage, the teachers in the distance were all standing at the fence of the school, wondering why the pupils were late for class, thinking that someone was inciting them. Once I had finished, all the students scampered off towards the classroom at the high school and I followed, as they had pleaded with me to come and speak to the headmaster. Unfortunately, he was not there, but I chatted to the vice-head and agreed to return the next day.

The next morning, Carol and I returned to the high school. We were welcomed and greeted most warmly by the vice-headmistress. She then sounded the bell, and many hundreds of the black students gathered. I explained what God had called me to do in carrying the cross and bowl throughout the nation, and shared the gospel with them. To our great joy, many responded and Carol and I stood with a long queue of young folk, praying for them one by one as they came up to us. There were so many of them, we could not do each one justice, but our hearts were overwhelmed as we headed back from the school, knowing that Jesus had touched the hearts of so many teenagers. Being out on the road alone again after that seemed almost strange, having been with such a multitude of people and ministering to so many of them.

Our family's first move was to the little village of Mount Ayliff where we stayed at a very primitive and poor black mission. It was strange to be the only white people in the town and the recipients of stares from the local community wherever we went. We found we were on a rapid learning curve, with our cultural values and sense of privacy being speedily adjusted. For example, we would try to sit outside the caravan only to find twenty people within three metres of us, simply sitting and staring all day long. We would try to eat but feel too embarrassed in front of these hungry people. Not having enough food for them all we would retreat inside the caravan and close the door, only to find twenty black noses pressed against the window staring at us.

Compounding the issue was the fact that, as I tried to spend time with the Lord alone, the only private place was the car. Opening my eyes after prayer, I would be greeted by twenty pairs of eyes gazing at close range at me through the windows of the car. We couldn't chase them away because that would undermine the very thing that God had brought us to this place for and so gradually we learned to endure as God moulded our characters.

We had a delightful time in and around Mount Ayliff. I would often spend the days out on the road with the cross and bowl, then minister at the little mission both morning and night to the crowds that gathered there. My walk then took me on towards Mount Frere and through to Qumbu. It was lovely greeting folk and chatting to them as I trudged along the twisty road that wove its way up and down through the Transkei.

A wonderful moment occurred one morning, when after journeying some ten kilometres, I saw a group of people outside one of the huts. I went across to them, we started chatting and they warmly invited me in. The house immediately filled with people, mainly men, and one of them began interpreting for me. It was such a joy to see them in so heartfelt a way surrender their lives to the Lord as I was able to wash their feet and show them the servant-love of Jesus. These are the moments I love out on the road, just being at the roadside and bringing Jesus to others. I often feel that in the church we talk Jesus so much but don't often live Jesus to others. My frequent prayer is, 'Lord, make me like you; Lord, make me like you; you are a servant, make me one too.'

While walking in this rural and often primitive setting, the Lord started to speak to me about his power. He showed me that often the church and Christians seem to lack the power of God. The Holy Spirit began to etch the words of the Apostle Paul into my very being: 'The kingdom of God does not consist in words but in power' (1 Cor 4:20). As I sought the Lord about this, I started to learn about the dimensions of this power. I sensed the Lord saying that resources are stored by

accumulation. Jesus was explicit about this when he told
the parable of the talents and showed the severe consequences to those who were bad stewards of what the
Holy Spirit makes available to us (Mt 15:14–20). As we
read the Bible, pray and hear biblical teaching, resources
are, as it were, accumulated within us. Once we have
them, we have a responsibility to use them correctly—
or dire consequences result.

If we utilise the resources that Jesus has put within
us, we will find we are led into an active Christian walk.
Conversely, if we do not utilise the power of God made
available to us, we are led into a passive state in our
Christian life. This passive state has two paths that both
have the same result. The first is that as we allow the
power of the Holy Spirit to remain dormant in our lives,
it leads to a declining, then a decaying which in turn
leads to death in a spiritual sense. Have you ever
watched a tomato on a shelf in your kitchen over a
number of days? First it goes soft, then it goes rotten as
it decays and finally 'dies'.

The second path of passivity leads to fermenting and
a build-up of pressure. This, in turn, leads to an
explosion of frustration which also results in death. I
once remember being in a restaurant where a man
ordered a bottle of tomato ketchup. As he was about to
remove the lid it shot off, with a blast of tomato sauce
spraying people at the next three tables. In much the
same way, in churches that do not allow themselves to
be good stewards of God's power, fermentation ensues.
The pressure of frustration and gossip builds up,
resulting in an eventual explosion and spiritual hurt and
death for both individuals and the church.

While God was revealing this to me, true to his
unfailing faithfulness, he honoured me in providing me
with a lovely Spirit-filled young Xhosa interpreter by the
name of Vile (pronounced Vee-lay). He was truly
articulate and able to interpret well and accurately. The
first morning I was out on the road with Vile I asked
God to apply the principles that he was teaching me. I

asked him to do something special and allow his stored power to become active, enhancing and life-giving to bless Vile that day.

We hadn't been out on the road long before we found ourselves chatting to a small crowd of folk and washing one or two pairs of feet. While this was taking place, a man asked if I ever went into the huts to pray for people.

'Why do you ask?' I responded.

He explained that his wife was very ill and pointed out his hut, way off in the distance. I explained that we could not go immediately, but promised to return later that day. After this delightful start to the day we journeyed on down into the little town of Qumbu. I have never before or since experienced what took place there. As we entered its bustling outskirts, all of a sudden a crowd spotted me, rushed towards me and started mobbing me as I was giving out stickers and sharing the love of Jesus. As I tried to walk, the crowd grew and grew to the point where it was almost impossible to move, and they pushed me in a zigzag fashion along the main street. Eventually in desperation I got to an open stand and climbed onto a large rock where I began preaching with Vile interpreting. Under the power of the Holy Spirit we made an appeal and many hundreds surrendered their lives to the Lord in that place. I knew that I could never wash everyone's feet so I chose a man and a woman from the crowd and washed their feet, as it were by proxy, for all who had given their lives to the Lord. We then moved into the town. I was promptly relieved of every Bible that I was carrying, and our supply of 'walking with Jesus' stickers also ran out. Later in the day we finally headed back to the little hut that I had promised to visit up in the hills.

The mud hut was a typical rural Transkeian dwelling. The floor, made from a mixture of compacted mud and cow dung, was dusty and dirty and there was a section on one side of the room where cooking took place over a smoky open fire. On the floor lay a lady breast-feeding her baby. The lady told us in Xhosa that she could not move as her left leg and arm were totally paralysed. Vile and I half-lifted and half-dragged her across to a battered chair. I put both her feet in the bowl and as I washed her feet, I called down the energising, healing, life-giving, accumulated power of the Holy Spirit to touch and heal her.

I dried her feet and instantly she jumped up and started dancing around, triggering ecstatic jubilation in the other two women in the hut. All five of us danced around rejoicing and celebrating before God. We then took a picture of her standing outside the hut holding her baby on the arm that had previously been paralysed, and headed back to the caravan. Upon our return, Vile could not contain himself, but ran ahead of me shouting and exclaiming to Carol, telling her with effervescent joy all that God had done. God had answered my prayer, and blessed this young interpreter on his first day out on the road with me.

I love the way the Lord can cause the most amusing things to happen. One night while we were in Qumu we organised a meeting in a large tin barn situated on one of the local farms. We don't normally do this but as there were no churches we decided to gather the folk together. After the meeting, a young girl was brought to me. She had had a very severe case of polio in her right leg, wore irons and her boot was built up at least twenty centimetres (eight inches).

As they brought her to me, the withering of my faith was almost comparable to the withered leg before me. I cried out to God for her healing, not having much faith to exercise at all, when suddenly I opened my eyes and saw the built-up boot protruding far beyond the sole of the other shoe. Amid much acclamation and glory to Jesus, I struggled with my own disbelief at what had just happened and asked her to come to our caravan later the next day to confirm that her healing was real and that God had indeed touched her.

On my return from the road the following evening, the young lady was waiting outside the caravan. One of

The woman who was healed of paralysis in the Transkei.

the funniest sights I have ever seen greeted my eyes. As she stood chatting to me, it was as if she had her foot on a huge step. Looking down, I noticed the problem was that she still had her eight-inch built-up shoe on what was now a normal length leg. I told her that she needed to go back to the hospital and ask them to check to see whether she needed any built-up shoe at all. My family and Vile roared with joyful laughter as she appeared to pole-vault off on her built-up shoe into the distance. Praise God, who is truly our healer.

From Qumbu I headed towards Umtata, a fairly modern, bustling city and capital of the Transkei. As I approached the city I began asking God, as I always do for big cities, 'Lord is there anything for Umtata?' As I walked and prayed I sensed a clear answer: 'Yes, David, I have brought you here to see one man.' I enquired, 'Lord, who is that?' and the reply came: 'His name is Major General Bantu Holomisa.' I said, 'Lord, that will have to be a miracle, because I don't know a single soul in the whole of Umtata.' By now the Lord had taught me to trust him, and everything he had spoken to me since he first started calling me to the road had come to pass. On arriving in Umtata, I came into contact with the most lovely, caring group of Baptist women who prayed. I shared with them what God had shown me for Umtata and they began praying.

Not very long afterwards, a lady I had only recently met came to the house where we had parked the caravan and escorted me to the Bothasigcau Building, which is the home of the Transkeian Government and Administration. On my arrival I was taken to the Protocol, where a man questioned me for at least twenty minutes. At the end of that time, he asked me to come to the top storey with him. I was then introduced to a very kind man by the name of Captain Xaba, who turned out to be General Holomisa's secretary. After chatting with me for twenty minutes, he asked if I would return at 2.30 that afternoon to meet with the military ruler of this tiny nation of three million people.

I went and prayed before returning at two o'clock to the government headquarters. I was ushered through a rather elaborate entrance into a beautiful panelled office to meet Major General Holomisa, the head of the Transkeian government. He entered, neatly dressed in an elegant black suit, and drew his chair around to the same side of his very large desk. We chatted about what God had brought me to Umtata for. I explained to him that the Bible instructs us to pray for our leaders and heads of state, and that in accordance with God's word, I had come to pray with him. After twenty minutes he mentioned that he was under pressure as he had to meet the foreign minister of another country in seven minutes' time. He said that he really wanted to hear what I had to say and asked if I would mind returning the next day to continue my discussion with him. I departed, thanking God that long before we started, he had told us that we would touch the poor and the powerful, and that he had brought this meeting to pass.

The next morning I prayerfully prepared my heart before going back to the government building. I was ushered into his luxurious office, where this time he was dressed in his military uniform. I was able to show General Holomisa from Romans 13 that there is no authority except from God and that those who wield authority are established by God. I explained that he was in power for no other reason but to give honour to God and to bring God's purposes to those over whom he ruled. I said that although he thought that he had seized the country through a coup, it was in fact God who had put him in power. As I went on, I felt convinced that that night Carol would be picking me up on the border with my bags!

We also talked about the difficulties facing one who rules and how the buck has to stop at the head of state. He shared that it was often not easy to make the right decisions, for in pleasing one he would always offend another, and we reflected that leadership was a lonely place. I told him that all wisdom and knowledge came from the fear of God according to God's word, and said that if he wanted true wisdom in making decisions for his nation it would only come as he yielded his life to God.

As I sat with my Bible I was also able to show him in the Scriptures that Jesus said in Matthew 10:32: 'Everyone . . . who shall confess Me before men I will also confess him before My Father who is in heaven. But whoever shall deny Me before men, I will also deny him before My Father who is in heaven.' I charged the General before Almighty God to confess Jesus before the nation in his forthcoming Republic Day celebration speech in Umtata. He told me that he would consider this. I then explained to him that the people of the land saw him as a servant, but that Jesus was the greatest servant of all and that I had come with that servant-love of Jesus, and asked him if he would allow me the privilege of washing his feet. He graciously agreed to this and I washed his feet in the privacy of his office with Jesus as witness. As I knelt to wash his feet, I questioned him about his relationship with the Lord. Once we had finished praying together, he called his secretary Captain Xaba into the office who took a photograph before I left.

As I stopped to pick up my cross, I felt God reminding me, 'Have I not promised that my word will never return void?' I thanked God as I left that I had had the privilege of delivering God's word in uncompromising fashion to this man. I thanked the Lord that he had been confronted with God's word and heard God's word, and for the privilege of being his humble servant. That night my prayer was, 'Thank you, Lord, that you have chosen to use us in the way that you do. Thank you, Lord, that we can be your servants to your servants, to the lowly and the peasants, to the poor and the outcasts and to men in high places. Be glorified, Lord; guide our feet and guide our paths to your glory.'

A few afternoons later, we had the pleasure and privilege of arriving at the small settlement of Lujizweni.

I say 'privilege', because we were to discover that God
had used this little place in such a powerful way, as they
had experienced revival continually for the past six years.
Lujizweni is rural and by many standards primitive, yet
God chooses to use whom he will and I thank God for
his presence that we saw there. Truly we saw the church
in action as seldom we had seen before. The church is
pastored by a dear brother called Joseph Kobo, who has
been mightily used by God. Joseph is a humble man and
claims no credit for himself in any way for all that God
has done there, where they have seen miracles and acts
comparable to those of the early church.

We spent our first afternoon sitting chatting to Joseph
and his lovely wife Mabel, simply learning about all that
God was doing in Lujizweni. We had decided not to
bring our caravan with us because we wanted to identify
with the local people and live with them, experiencing
their hardships and the primitive way in which they live,
and we thanked God that he was teaching us just that,
to his glory. Word had gone out very quickly that we
were there and in the late afternoon people were already
starting to arrive for us to minister to them. We prayed
for a little boy with a badly deformed hand and foot and
Carol and I wept as we washed his limbs.

One of the things that overwhelmed us was the joyous
giving hearts of these people, despite the hardship under
which they live. We had water brought to us to wash
our hands after we arrived, only to find out that they
had to walk in pouring rain to the river to fetch it. They
had no toilet facilities and no lights, but they cooked for
us and served us and waited upon us hand and foot.
We felt unworthy of all this, but we saw the true church
in action. We stayed in a home near Joseph's hut and
other ladies came to the place where we were staying
simply to cook for us and serve us.

The first evening we had the joy of going to one of
their Bible meetings through the mud and slush of the
primitive roads. Although these meetings had been
going on there for five years, the place was packed and

we gathered that they had met seven days a week for praise and worship, 365 days a year for all that time. On our way home late that night, we saw many who had to walk many kilometres through the twisting hills and muddy roads to reach their huts in the freezing rain. We couldn't help wondering what type of pseudo-Christianity so much of the western church lives in, when this primitive Christianity truly knows what it means to count the cost. During the meeting that night we prayed for many to be healed, and that God would touch them, and saw a young girl's ears healed of deafness. A man's kidneys were also healed and we thanked God for all that he was doing in that place to his glory.

The next morning we were awakened by our dear hostess Margaret tapping on the door with a cup of tea for us. In normal circumstances that would seem a fairly ordinary thing, but it was pouring with rain. We realised it had meant slipping and sliding about in mud, going to the river to fetch water, collecting wood, making a fire, preparing tea and then walking through the rain to bring it to where we were staying. I thanked God for the testimony of these Christians, for their servant-heartedness. One young lady had in fact walked back from the meeting the previous night, a distance of some four kilometres, to make us tea before we went to bed, after which she would have had to walk several kilometres in the rain up a muddy country path back to her hut. After we rose the next morning, the folk brought us heated water in buckets. Once we had washed, we headed across to Joseph's dwelling to have breakfast with him and Mabel. The women had prepared a western-style breakfast for us, not wanting us to be subjected to the hardship of their staple diet. We wished that they hadn't made such a fuss of us, although of course we appreciated it, but we felt unworthy to receive it.

As we sat chatting to Joseph, I was to discover that morning in that humble little place many things that I believe could be an example to the body of Christ worldwide. I noticed several rooms filled with people in a mud building on his property and asked Joseph what it was. He said, 'Oh, those people have come here for prayer.'

'What is wrong with them?'

'They are sick,' Joseph replied.

I asked him how long they would be there, who supported them, and where they came from. He said, 'They come from all over the Transkei, and the church feeds and supports them; they stay there until they get better and then return home.' At this, my heart leapt. I could hardly believe what I was hearing. What a positive statement to the world—that people would come to a 'prayer hospital' and have the whole man ministered to. No grandeur about it, just mud huts, and people living in primitive conditions supported by a primitive church that has no money. Surely, I thought, God must honour this. I just prayed quietly, 'Thank you, Lord; you are teaching me so much.'

Next we heard about the rondawel (hut) where this mighty revival had begun, where women of God had prayed and fasted for thirty days without food or water. In their primitive state, no one had told them that you need to drink water while you are fasting, but none of them had died. We heard too about people who had been raised from the dead, Joseph modestly sharing all this with us. He said that the one woman who was raised had been brought in several days after dying. Her body had already started to decompose and there was a stench of death. I couldn't help thinking how the Lord had called Lazarus, already dead for four days, from the tomb and realised that the first-hand power of God was permeating the very lives of these primitive people.

I asked to see the hut where the revival had begun and was somewhat disappointed to find that there were people living in it. Carol and I were then introduced to Joseph's old mother-in-law who had been used to instigate the revival under the power of the Holy Spirit.

A simple illiterate peasant woman, she had received a message from the Holy Spirit, acted upon it and the revival began. I felt I should prophesy over her, and said that the room was to be cleared and returned to a place of prayer and that people would come from all over the world to pray in this mud hut where God had done so many mighty things and from which so much had grown. I gave the place where people convalesced a new name; I said it was to be called the 'Prayer Hospital' and they rejoiced at that. I thanked God for allowing me to encounter it, to see in the Spirit what he would continue to do. I thanked God for the hundreds of people who would stream from this nation and the world to continue to pray in this primitive place where God chooses to move. I was mindful that God used a manger in which to lay his Son, simple and lowly. I prayed, 'God, come and take your glory in this place.'

The rain never abated in all the days that we were there, and on the last night in the meeting, I washed Joseph's feet while Carol washed Mabel's. As the Holy Spirit gave us anointing, we called people out with ailments and saw them healed. One lady spoke of how she had been healed of deafness during our time there, that she had come to meetings before and all she could do was watch the people dance and sing and could never hear the words, but that God had touched and healed her deafness and that she was now free. All I could say was, 'Thank you, God, for all that you do; be glorified, be glorified, be glorified.'

On the day when we finally left Lujizweni, Joseph insisted on accompanying us along the extremely muddy road which led back to Umtata. Many times our car slid along the road sideways, and on more than one occasion we found ourselves totally bogged down in the mud. The locals would help us dislodge the car and we would have another go at getting through. At one stage it seemed impossible: the car just would not get through the mud despite several attempts. Crowds of people would help push us out, we would try valiantly again only to bog down completely once more. Eventually Joseph, with his incredible mountain-driving skills, took the wheel of my car and came flying through the mud with the rest of us slithering knee-deep behind, trying to push, and finally we succeeded. We went joyously on our way, bumping back towards Umtata.

Once there, we headed towards the home of Supreme Court Judge Colin White and his wife Erica. By this stage, they had become good friends of ours, and had taken us into the shelter of their beautiful home which had become a sanctuary to us. Erica, a refined but most efficient lady, stared in disbelief at our mud-clogged motor car, which looked as if it had just been on the 'Roof of Africa' rally. She immediately armed herself with a stick and hosepipe, and started prising the mud from beneath the car and the mudguards, hosing our car down and restoring it to its pristine condition.

The reason for our having pressed on with such determination to get back to Umtata, was that I was due that night to address a ladies' meeting to be hosted by the president's wife at the palace in Umtata. Several prominent men had also been invited to the meeting, among whom was the Chief Justice and his wife, Judge White and his wife, as well as medical doctors and other professional people. We were assembled in a reception room in the palace enjoying a cup of tea, when much to our surprise we were called to attention as President Ndamase and the First Lady entered the room. I was deeply honoured as I was told that this was the first time that the president had ever attended one of these meetings.

The palace was plush beyond description, with banqueting halls and boardrooms flowing off each wing. The room we had originally been ushered into had some seventy beautiful upholstered chairs arranged in semi-circles, facing a table laden with food and tea for our benefit. Once we had had our refreshments, the president asked us to move through to the room where we were to hold the meeting. We went down a long passage to another room equally as plush, with two important-looking chairs resembling thrones behind the

With Maj. Gen. Bantu Holomisa, military ruler of the Transkei.

table at the head of the room. Each person was seated by the Protocol, and I was ushered to the front to one of the throne-like chairs where I sat down feeling rather conspicuous to say the least. All the ladies were dressed up to the nines and all the men had suits on. I was wearing my usual 'Jesus-washed feet' T-shirt and my denim jacket and felt distinctly out of place.

It was extremely hot, and after a little singing and a short prayer, I was asked to preach. I commenced by asking the president if he had any objection to my removing my jacket. The atmosphere was incredibly tense and awkward and everyone was stumbling and stammering, but I thank the Holy Spirit that he eventually broke down the stiffness, people became relaxed and I was able to proclaim God's word truly under the anointing of his grace. I had thought that the president might not stay for the sermon, but he listened intently.

At the end, I made an appeal for people to live uncompromising lives before Jesus, and almost the whole room came forward, led by the Chief Justice, the Protocol people, those who had been waiting on us and all and sundry. What a glorious night! I asked the president and his wife to sit down on the two throne-like chairs and requested the privilege of washing their feet, which I duly did. I explained to them that as a man and woman of prayer and the mother and father of the nation, they were training their children—the citizens of their nation—in the way that they should go. I assured them that this was God's promise from his word to them. Then the Holy Spirit struck. As I started prophesying over people, many fell under the power of the Spirit and chairs went flying—all this happening under the president's bright-eyed gaze—but I chuckled to myself and thought, 'God, you have your way in all places.'

People were overjoyed at what happened that night. As we left triumphantly, we thanked God for all that he had done in the spiritual realm. We thanked the Lord that once again he was fulfilling his promise to us that we would touch the poor and the powerful, whether in mud huts or palaces.

6

The Golden Lampstand

The sun blazed down as, well equipped with water tanks
and Bibles, I walked along in the country carrying the
cross and bowl. I had a spring in my step as I walked
on South African soil once more. It had taken us some
two-and-a-half months to weave our way through the
Transkei. Once we had got within striking distance of
the border, I moved the family to the tiny little Eastern
Cape town of Komga because of the lack of public
facilities where we were. Despite the Transkei's primitive
environment, we had truly experienced the hand of God
there. It had been good, too, to visit my birthplace. Sadly
run-down now, and in a bad state of disrepair, the village
nevertheless tugged at my heart-strings. It was a
moment of pure nostalgia to stand at the place of my
earthly roots, knowing that I now have heavenly roots
in a house not made with human hands.

With the family now ensconced in Komga, I had
moved back and forth for several days through the Kei
border post on the boundary between Transkei and
South Africa. Inevitably during my travels across the
border each day, the customs officials and officers had
become interested in my progress, and on the day that
I finally reached the border post there was much light-
hearted enthusiasm over the accomplishment. It had
been an incredibly rainy day and I resembled the
proverbial drowned rat. As I entered the building there
was a long queue of people waiting to have their
documents processed, and as I stood in the queue the

folk gathered round questioning me about what had
happened during my time in the Transkei. There was
great excitement as I was able to witness to God's
faithfulness and all the good things that he had done
during my time in this little country.

Eventually it was my turn to have my papers
processed. The routine at the border post after showing
one's passport, is that one generally declares the number
of people in one's car and the car's registration. One
then receives a slip of paper with the number of
passengers, the registration of the car and an official
Republic of South Africa customs entry stamp. As I stood
at the counter, the customs man greeted me warmly and
then held me up for some time as he got busy with pen
and paper. Finally, with a big smile on his face, he proudly
handed me a slip of paper which had a stick figure of the
well-known television character the Saint with a halo
upon its head, no registration, just W for walking and
'Persons: 1', all legalised with an official South African
entry stamp. I laughed and gave glory to God, while the
customs officials and the crowd bade me farewell.

As I looked beyond the barrier on the other side of
the border, I could see the familiar sight of a blue
Mercedes Benz with Carol and Ronnie-Russ standing in
the pouring rain, waiting to welcome me. As I stepped
across the border post, I hoisted the cross and bowl high
above my head and as a family we glorified Jesus, much
to the bewilderment of passing motorists. God once
again in his faithfulness had protected me along the
highways and byways where people often told me they
were too scared to drive for fear of being hijacked. Yet
I had come through this dangerous setting step by step
each day for two-and-a-half months knowing only the
protecting hand of Jehovah El Shaddai—my God who
is more than enough.

Now I was back in the Eastern Cape on a beautiful
sunny day, walking through the rolling hills, sometimes
catching the waft of the sharp kraal smell peculiar to that
part of the country. I love the rugged thorn-bush terrain

which has a beauty all its own, and every now and then I would catch the tangy scent that comes from the beautiful pineapple plantations that grace the hills of this part of the sub-continent. Ahead of me lay one of our major cities—a seaport situated on a river—East London. Not the London situated on the Thames, but a populous South African town sprawled north and south of the Buffalo river and lapped by the Indian Ocean. As I moved towards it, my mind was set on the city and God's will for it.

'Lord,' I asked, 'is there a strategy for East London?' Immediately a picture flashed before me of the golden lampstand in the prophecy of Zechariah. Zechariah himself could not initially understand the vision, and it certainly appeared to me to have no significance to my particular situation. The next day, while out on the road, I asked the Lord again about East London. Yet again the lampstand picture flashed into my mind, with these accompanying verses:

And He said to me [Zechariah], 'What do you see?' And I said, 'I see, and behold, a lampstand all of gold, with its bowl on the top of it, and its seven lamps on it with seven spouts belonging to each of the lamps which are on the top of it; also two olive trees by it . . .' (Zech 4:2–3).

And I answered the second time and said to Him, 'What are the two olive branches which are beside the two golden pipes, which empty the golden oil from themselves?' So He answered me saying, 'Do you not know what these are?' And I said, 'No, My Lord.' Then He said, 'These are the two anointed ones, who are standing by the Lord of the whole earth' (Zech 4:12–14).

I could not work out why every time I asked the Lord about East London he showed me this golden lampstand. After all, I pondered, I knew this chapter well, having preached on it several times. Then the Holy Spirit brought revelation. He focused my attention on the two golden pipes which emptied the golden oil from themselves. The Lord reminded me that one pipe had been symbolic of Joshua who was the anointed one of the whole earth, the spiritual leader of his time. The other pipe stood for Zerubbabel, who was the civic leader of the time, and God brought the two of them to glorify his temple. Clearly in my spirit the Lord said, 'I am going to do this in East London. I am going to bring together the civic and the spiritual leaders to glorify my name, doing what will bring a testimony of my mighty hand in the city and beyond.'

As Carol and I prayed and fasted over the next days, God began to reveal to us his plan in more complete detail, as he confirmed through his word what he was preparing for the city of East London. We clearly saw that the pipe which stood for the civic leader represented the mayor and knew that the other pipe represented spiritual leadership. We felt God was calling us to bring the mayor and a spiritual leader together for an extended period of prayer for the city, which God would use as a prophetic statement to break the strongholds of bondage that had so long existed over the city. As we prayed we felt that God wanted to bring revival in three ways: *spiritually*, *civically* and *economically* to the city.

Confirmation came through the prophecy that immediately precedes the one about the golden lampstand, where it says, '"In that day," declares the Lord of hosts, "every one of you will invite his neighbour to sit under his vine and under his fig tree"' (Zech 3:10). Our hearts leapt for joy as we realised that the fig tree and the vine were symbolic of the Holy Place. We believed that the mayor and the spiritual leader should come together to pray on the sea-front for the city each day, and they in turn would each invite their neighbours to come to that holy place that God was anointing on the sea-front. As we thought about it, it seemed almost impossible. How would this ever happen, how would this miracle occur, when I hardly knew a single soul within the borders of East London? How would I convince men with such busy schedules, when I didn't know them, and they had never heard of me, to take part in this radical twelve-day spiritual exercise?

We continued to wait on the Lord, and then after some days came the final confirmation, a verse that 'came alive' for us even as we read it: 'Now He who supplies seed to the sower and bread for food, will supply and *multiply your seed for sowing* and increase the harvest of your righteousness' (2 Cor 9:10, italics mine). We believed that God was saying that the mayor and the man who would be symbolic of spiritual leadership would be seed, and that God would multiply that seed for the sowing and the increase of his harvest. Verse 11 goes on, 'You will be enriched in everything for all liberality, which through us is producing thanksgiving to God.' We knew that as the people of East London started to see what God would do, the result would be thanksgiving to God. Verse 12 continues, 'For the ministry of this service is not only fully supplying the needs of the saints but is also overflowing through many thanksgivings to God.'

In what lay ahead we were to see both believers and unbelievers having their needs met out of what was born in prayer as we acted in obedience to God's word. And then God finally spoke to us through verse 13: 'Because of the proof given by this ministry [which was to take place in East London] they will glorify God for your obedience to your confession of the gospel of Christ, and for the liberality of your contribution to them and to all.' Hallelujah! We now knew clearly that God had spoken, but the big question was where to begin. Little did we realise that we were being led into one of the greatest spiritual battles we were ever to face on the road, and that there was to be much spiritual warfare before this thing that God had so clearly spoken to us could come to pass.

By God's grace the first couple we were to meet in East London was the ex-Springbok cricket captain, Trevor Goddard, and his gracious wife Lesley, who were later to become dear friends of Carol's and mine. The Goddards immediately invited us to their lovely home which enjoys a magnificent view, looking down on the Nahoon river as it winds towards the sea.

Trevor had become a Christian after his career as an international cricketer, which earned him the acclaim of being one of the all-time greats. As we shared lunch that day, we exchanged stories of the goodness of the Lord's dealings in both our lives, as well as sharing our feelings about the joys and challenges of public ministry. I did not feel able that day to mention anything to Trevor about what God had been revealing to me about East London, but as we departed and headed back to our caravan, I felt that in some way Trevor would play a significant role in what lay ahead. Our time was then abruptly interrupted by two conferences that we had to fly elsewhere for, both speaking engagements that I had committed myself to some months before. Ten days later we came back to experience one of the most intense periods of spiritual warfare we had ever known.

Upon our return I decided that I would contact Trevor Goddard immediately to share with him what God had shown me. I called his house and was told by one of his daughters that her dad was in hospital. I found this rather strange and alarming as Trevor had been in excellent health when I had last seen him some two weeks previously. I phoned again later that night and managed to speak to Lesley who informed me that Trevor was in hospital with a serious gangrenous wound in one leg as a result of an accident some days before. Immediately I headed towards the hospital to pray for him, hoping that I might have an opportunity to share what God had laid on my heart. But to no avail: the hospital ward was crowded with friends and fellow pastors as well as a journalist trying to persuade Trevor to write an article for him.

I did not understand what was going on. I had been so sure that Trevor had a role to play, and now he was lying in hospital with gangrene in his leg. I had lost two more days and was feeling increasingly frustrated. The next day I called Lesley and shared with her what I felt God had been saying. She graciously encouraged me even though she was under pressure at the time through

Trevor's predicament. Once again, my hopes were raised as they said that they might well be able to treat Trevor's wound and release him from hospital within a short space of time. This, however, was not to be and my hopes were further dashed over the next few days as we realised that Trevor would have to have an operation. I could in no way understand what God was doing, but the situation seemed to be getting worse.

During these days I decided to focus my attention instead on the man who would be symbolic of spiritual leadership in this venture. Over the few weeks that I had been in and around East London, I had had the privilege of meeting and preaching in the church of Derek Crumpton, a highly respected man of God in South Africa and in many different parts of the world. Derek and his wife Jean received Carol and me with much love and graciousness and we were truly thankful for the friendship that God was bringing about with them. Derek was the logical choice to be symbolic of spiritual leadership as he was in fact already that to many around the country, but somehow I felt the Lord restraining me, saying no, in this instance it was to be another.

As I waited on the Spirit, I sensed God showing me that it was to be a man by the name of Chris Venter, the pastor of the Christian Centre, whom I had never met. I endeavoured to get hold of Chris. After numerous phone calls to his office, and discovering that his home telephone was unlisted, we reached a dead end. He always seemed to be out of town, in meetings, or away at conferences of some description. The situation seemed impossible. Doors were apparently closing on every side.

People whom I met and told about what God was saying for their city were frequently warm and encouraging but also rather sceptical about the role that the mayor was to play. Often they laughed openly at the possibility that he might even begin to contemplate coming to pray on the sea-front. One group even said to me, 'If you meet him, take along some soap and wash his mouth out, as he has actually been rebuked by the press for the language that he uses in public.' These comments did nothing to uplift my already rather battered faith with regard to seeing God's plan come to pass. I felt spiritually oppressed, depressed—although I am not normally depressive—and attacked by the unrestrained powers of hell. We prayed with seemingly no answer forthcoming, feeling at our wits' end.

One morning on Gonubie beach I was crying out to the Lord, not understanding why I was in this extreme battle, when suddenly the Lord showed me that he was allowing me to walk through the fire. He was checking me out to ensure that I loved the God of victory more than the victory of God. The Lord was to give me one last promise and then one last test of surrender. The promise was from Haggai 2:19: 'Is the seed still in the barn? Even including *the vine*, *the fig tree*, the pomegranate, and the olive tree, it has not borne fruit. Yet from this day on I will bless you' (italics mine). Then came the test. The Lord directed me to the scripture, 'Direct your mind to the highway, the way by which you went' (Jer 31:21). Once again, he was clearly saying to me, 'Walk on.'

I sat stunned in disbelief. I prayed out loud and said, 'Lord, I am sure that I have heard you about East London, but if I am to be a fool to all the people that I have shared with, then I am prepared to be a fool and acknowledge that I have missed it.' That day in simple obedience I picked up my cross and bowl and started to walk out of East London. It was again like Abraham going with Isaac to the altar, knowing that God had blessed him and given him the gift, yet being prepared to give it back to God. Then, just as God intervened when Abraham lifted the knife to slay the child, so he intervened on our behalf. That night as I returned to the caravan, I received a message to say that Trevor Goddard had made an appointment for me to meet the mayor. Suddenly, I sensed that God was breaking through with a glimmer of hope and encouragement and a promise of ultimate victory. The battle is always most intense at the birth of a vision. Now at last I felt the intense cloud starting to lift.

Some days later, Carol and I found ourselves being ushered into the mayoral chamber of the city of East London. The mayor, an exceptionally large man, was accompanied by one of the city councillors. As I shared, he listened cautiously and politely and I thought, 'Lord, how ridiculous this must seem naturally-speaking to a man in his position.' But our Lord is indeed Jehovah Shammah—the God who is already there—and as we chatted, I saw the mayor starting to leaf through his diary to see when he could find twelve days to pray with me on the sea-front each morning. He told me he would not be able to do it that month as it was already December, which socially is their busiest time of the year, with the onslaught of holiday-makers from around the country. He did however say that he would be able to do it after the first week of January. I assured him that I believed that God had initiated all this and that out of obedience, I would be prepared to return.

Then came what seemed at the time to be another obstacle. He and his fellow councillor explained that they would need to seek the permission of the city council to allow the mayor to participate in such an event. My heart sank, my emotions raced, as I felt that this was just an excuse to fob me off. I chose however to keep my gaze fixed on the Lord. Carol and I left the elegant mayoral chamber and headed down the street, not knowing what to think, but also knowing that the things that are impossible with man are possible with God. Some days later I picked up the legendary *Daily Despatch* newspaper and there, to my astonishment and delight, I read a front-page headline which said, 'Mayor agrees to pray.' Carol and I hastily read the article, our eyes almost tripping over each word with excitement as we danced around and knew that the battle was the Lord's.

Now that God had secured the civic leader to be part of his plan, it seemed ridiculous that we had not been able to settle what we believed God had said regarding

a spiritual leader. Once again, I decided to cease from
striving and simply lay it in the Lord's lap. I had already
said to Carol that if ever I met Chris Venter it would
have to be God's doing, because I had done all that I
could in my own strength. Once again, God in his
faithfulness was to intervene. We were relaxing at the
home of the local TBN station manager and his wife,
Bernhard and Hazel Roebert, when suddenly the phone
rang and I was told the call was for me. The voice on
the other end said, 'Hi Dave, my name is Chris Venter.
I would truly love to meet you.' I could hardly believe
my ears and made an appointment to meet Chris in his
office later that afternoon.

As I sat in Chris' office and shared what God had laid
on my heart, telling him all that had happened, tears
welled up in his eyes. He pulled a list out of his drawer
and showed me the three things that he was praying for
each week: revival in the *spiritual, civic* and *economic*
life of the city. Precisely what God had laid on our hearts!
Chris then informed me that during the proposed
period, he was due to be away on holiday, but that he
so clearly believed that this was of God that he was
prepared to cut his holiday in half to be back in time for
the moment of commencement.

The Christmas and New Year period seemed to drag
and the days limped by before I was able to return to
East London with much excitement and expectancy in
my heart for what God was about to do. Finally the day
arrived: a Wednesday morning in early January, which
had been preceded by several days of false alarms. One
such alarm was a call I received from one of the city
councillors who expressed his misgivings concerning the
lack of advertising about what was to take place. He
wanted to know what media coverage and strategy had
been planned, as the city council was seeking as much
mileage out of this occasion as possible. I told him that
was just not the way I worked and that no advertising
or media coverage whatsoever had been planned;
instead I chose to place my trust in the Holy Spirit. I did

however feel incredibly pressurised, but sensed the Holy Spirit quietly saying to me, 'My ways are not the ways of man.'

My mind raced back to how David had tested King Saul's armour then discarded it in favour of five smooth stones and a sling, declaring to Goliath, 'You come to me with a sword, a spear and a javelin, but I come to you in the name of the Lord of hosts, the God of the armies of Israel, whom you have taunted' (1 Sam 17:45). The words of my singer/songwriter friend, Garth Hewitt, sprang to mind: 'I don't need your armour, I don't need your sword, I will put my trust in the power of the Lord.' The Lord showed me that the armour and the sword were the ways of men—the media, the press, television, etc. Another false alarm came the night before our first meeting, when I received a phone call from another city councillor who announced that the mayor was feeling a little apprehensive about the whole thing. My heart leapt; I thought, 'Oh no.' He then went on to say that because of the mayor's apprehension he didn't want to come on his own and would it be in order if the city councillor in question accompanied him?

As I headed in the early morning towards the Orient Beach, it was overcast and rainy, and my mind was pondering what might take place in the twelve days that lay ahead. As I reached the sea-front, the four of us all seemed to arrive simultaneously, Chris Venter, the mayor, the councillor and myself. We proceeded down towards the edge of the beach where the four of us stood huddled in the pouring rain under a golf umbrella. True to form, the Lord injected a moment of humour which helped break up the initial stiffness and formality of our prayers. A reporter from the *Daily Despatch* arrived to take a photograph of what he expected to be a rather magnificent prayer meeting conducted by the mayor on the sea-front. He asked where the meeting was and his face was an absolute picture when a rather embarrassed mayor emerged from beneath the large, dripping wet golf umbrella. Needless to say, the next morning there

was a large picture in the *Daily Despatch* of the four of
us standing beneath the umbrella.

God was, however, to bring about something special
that morning, as we started rebuking the enemy
strongholds that had held the city back. We addressed
the economic strongholds, the civic strongholds that had
dogged the previous city council and brought it into
disrepute over many years, and we spoke to the spiritual
strongholds and called upon the Holy Spirit to usher in
revival in that city. The next day we returned to find
that God had been faithful as each one 'brought his
neighbour to sit beneath the fig tree and the vine'. There
was far more than a doubling and the prayer meeting
started to gain momentum as we began to address many
different issues.

By the third day the crowd had grown so large that
we had to start using a public address system. The
following day with the crowd again doubled, we started
praising and worshipping, in the fervour of the Spirit of
God. It was glorious to see Catholics, Pentecostals, Faith
people, NG folk from the Dutch Reformed Church and
representatives of many other denominations standing
with linked hands in small groups dotted everywhere
as we prayed for the needs of the city of East London.
Surely these were days of revival as God was pouring
out his blessing. The press started to carry consistent
reports of what was happening, and word even got as
far as the city of Port Elizabeth. The headline in
their weekend paper read: 'EAST LONDONERS FLOCK TO
THE BEACHES TO PRAY'.

As we began each morning with praise and worship,
there would often be singing and praising in the Spirit,
handclapping and fervent prayer, much of which was
foreign to many of the churches represented. God in his
sovereignty, however, overruled and there was never
once any word of complaint, murmuring or offence taken
throughout the whole time, as we truly saw the body
of Christ coming together. Virtually every denomination
as well as people of all sectors of the community came

On East London's beachfront.

to experience this thing that God was doing in their midst. Some mornings we would pray specifically for the civic leaders, other mornings for the spiritual leaders. Each day we would pray for the homeless and the outcasts, and pray and stand against divorce, adultery and prostitution, and we saw God beginning to reach out as people came to pray and then got saved. We witnessed people who had not spoken to one another for years coming and linking hands as they prayed. We saw political opponents, arch-rivals, standing hand-in-hand praying for one another. Each morning we allowed people to divide into small groups of four or five as we brought need after need after need and let the groups intercede. Then we would pray corporately, then rejoice in the Lord; these were indeed glorious days when God was pouring out his Spirit in East London.

One morning I felt the need to pray for the leadership of the city as a whole, not isolated into separate compartments, so I requested all the civic leaders who were present—and there were several town councillors—as well as the many clergy, ministers, pastors and priests to come forward. I asked them to intersperse themselves and link arms to declare God's unity so that from that point on there wouldn't be a separate civic or spiritual leadership, but simply those who stood united as the fathers of the city. Truly as those men stood linked arm in arm, I once again saw the golden lampstand, and how God had joined the two pipes at the base to glorify his temple.

Before the twelve days were up we saw many prayers beginning to be answered. First, people came to salvation and that was exciting. Then we received word of businesses that had suddenly begun to prosper. One morning, the town council had asked us to pray for the urgent release of funds from central government for houses for many of the homeless coloured people on the outskirts of the city. I witnessed God's faithfulness in answering this prayer as I received an excited phone call from the mayor. He said that as he was driving towards his mayoral chamber that morning, he felt a clear leading from the Lord to ask the Town Treasurer to begin an investigation into a certain account. He said that as the Town Treasurer had done this, he had already found several million rand and believed that there were still millions to come. We shared this blessing with the people down on the sea-front and rejoiced at all that God was doing that day.

Some days before this magnificent season came to an end, Chris and I were prompted to take the mayor to lunch and to ask where he stood with Jesus. This resulted in the most glorious statement by him the following morning as he stood up and said, 'I declare to this city and these people present, that as for me and my household we love and will serve Jesus.' I stood with a heart filled with deep gratitude as Chris and I looked at each other, realising that the word says: 'If you confess with your mouth Jesus as Lord and believe in your heart that God raised Him from the dead, you shall be saved' (Rom 10:9).

The final Sunday morning was a time of high celebration and reflecting on the goodness of all that God had done during those days. A group of women told how they had always felt that God had been telling them to go and pray at the city gates, as strongholds that prevailed over the city had first entered there. They had never known, however, where those city gates were, but while we were praying at the Orient Beach, they realised that the first settlers who had come to the city had landed at that very spot. One of the ministers told how he had discovered on top of a wardrobe in his manse, a prophecy which had originated in Korea some seven years before. It came from people who didn't even know of the existence of East London in South Africa, but stated that God had said that he would light the flame of revival in East London. The minister felt that this could be the very moment.

As this wonderful time together came to a climax, I felt that I should wash the feet of the mayor and Chris, signifying God's cementing of the civic and the spiritual to glorify his name. The mayor in turn presented me with a crest of the city's emblem as well as a tie with the same emblem, and we ended by giving God glory for all that had been done during those days. Before our departure, Carol and I received the greatest reward possible, something that doubtless caused the angels in heaven to rejoice. A banquet was given at which forty ministers, pastors, priests, dominees and their wives from every different denomination were present. They all sat 'in one accord with one heart and glorified the God and Father of our Lord Jesus Christ'. Hallelujah! Love's redeeming work was done!

As I write this three years later, this revival is still in evidence as God continues to pour out his blessings on the city. Carol and I were invited to be guests at a day of thanksgiving convened by the subsequent Mayor of East London, who gave public recognition to 'the blessings of God' overtaking the city.

7
Help, It's a Ghost!

'I was very annoyed with you this morning, young man,' interjected an elderly lady as I was attempting to pray with her while washing her feet. The fact that she called me 'young man' endeared her to me immediately, but the cause of her annoyance was a mystery. Soon however my curiosity got the better of me. I stopped praying and enquired: 'Excuse me, ma'am, but why were you annoyed with me?'

'I came prepared for you to wash my feet this morning and you didn't.' I pondered this awhile. Generally, I only ever wash feet in a service if the Holy Spirit shows me I should. I certainly don't want to make a doctrine out of it or do it simply as a matter of course. That particular morning I hadn't been directed to wash any feet, so I didn't. In the evening it was different, and thus I found myself with this lady before me. But what exactly did she mean by her second statement?

'Er, excuse me, ma'am, but just how did you come . . . *prepared*?'

Without missing a beat, she replied, 'Well, you see, I put my pantihose on, and I cut the feet off.' A gale of laughter immediately swept through the congregation and I realised that, as I was still 'wired for sound' via a lapel microphone, the church's PA system had faithfully amplified our little interchange.

So often in the kingdom of God and out on the road, the unexpected springs itself upon one in the most unlikely places, and in the most delightful ways. I have come to learn that the unexpected doesn't necessarily have to be traumatic. It all depends on how we perceive it. Do we see and react with our natural minds or do we walk continually with the mind of Christ? Picture the disciples alone in the boat as, storm-tossed and battered by wind and waves, they attempted to row across the Sea of Galilee. Exhaustion and fear overcame them and they began to panic. Then into this already stressful situation came the wholly unexpected: a figure walking towards them across the sea.

Immediately they had to choose how to react: depend on God in the situation or trust to their natural instincts. Unfortunately, blinded by fear, the majority chose to keep their focus on the plight of the moment and reacted to the unexpected visitor with a panic-stricken shriek: 'Help, it's a ghost!' Peter, however, chose to see in the Spirit. Recognising Jesus walking towards them, he said, 'Lord, here I come'—and stepped out on the water. Most of us, in reading this story tend to remember that Peter then shifted his gaze to the natural—the wind and the waves—and began to sink. But the profound fact remains that while Peter kept his eyes on Jesus, *he walked on water*.

When the unexpected arises, we can either scream for help, or step out on water knowing our dependency and our need to keep our gaze fixed on Jesus. Every time I don the cross and bowl and head out onto the highways and byways, I realise that the unexpected awaits. In fact, each time I wash someone's feet in the streets, it is a total miracle of God. I realise that it is purely his anointing and his grace which he has bestowed upon me that allows people to let me wash their feet on the main street of a city. Imagine yourself, even as a Christian, meeting me on the street—and I ask to wash your feet. It's very public. Friends or family might see you sitting there without your shoes on, having your feet washed. Even worse, people from your work— colleagues or employees—might spot you. Or some folk from your sports club, or a dignitary you know. How will you react to their spoken or unspoken questioning later on? Yet the beautiful thing is that when the Holy Spirit speaks, it really doesn't matter who sees, or who passes, or where it is, because all these obstacles and barriers suddenly collapse. The amazing fact is that of the many thousands and thousands of people whose feet I have asked to wash, the number who have refused me can be counted on one hand.

I remember once seeing an interview with a well-known showbusiness celebrity who said that the greatest nightmare he could ever have would be to wake up and discover that his singing voice had gone. I guess similarly, if I were to have a nightmare, it would be to wake up one day and discover that God had lifted his hand of anointing from me, to find as I stepped out onto the streets with the cross and bowl that his Spirit no longer brought people under conviction as I showed them the servant-love of Christ. Each time I wash someone's feet out there it's a miracle of God, and with the apostle Paul I can truthfully say that 'I am what I am by the grace of God'.

A typical example of my utter dependency on the Holy Spirit occurred as I walked towards the town of Kokstad. Nestled in the hills with the tip of the Drakensberg mountain range looming in the distance, Kokstad is a quaint place with a personality all its own. Situated in Southern Natal, it is one of the main supply centres for traders who drive truck-load after truck-load of supplies into the Transkei. I had moved the family on ahead of me into the town and had already preached in some of the churches there. Then came the clear warning from some of the townsfolk who said: 'We don't care what has happened elsewhere on your journey; Kokstad is a cynical little town and people will never allow you to wash their feet here.' As I walked along the side of the road towards Kokstad, waving at motorists and greeting passers-by in the name of Jesus, a kaleidoscope of emotions and thoughts rushed through my mind, and as I strode along I prayed gently in the Spirit, just fixing my inner gaze upon Jesus.

Anyone who knows Kokstad, will remember that there is a great divide in the form of a railway track which crosses the main road into the town. The railway crossing is a hub of activity with a fair number of people hanging about for one reason or another. The railtrack is such a clear demarcation, that if you step over it you are in the town, and if you step back again, you are out of it. I could see the railway line ahead of me. I continued to pray in the Spirit as I approached it, then crossed it. As soon as I had stepped over the line, I noticed a car broken down at the side of the road. The sight that presented itself was somewhat comical. The bonnet was raised high in the air, and all that could be seen were the well-rounded rumps of two gentlemen with their heads buried in the engine and their feet dangling in mid-air. Walking across to the car, I joined by also sticking my head into the engine compartment and asking, 'Having problems?' Now it's not every day that a man with a cross and bowl sticks his head into your engine when it's broken down, and the result was the rapid exit of the aforesaid gentlemen from their confined quarters.

After a discussion about the plight of their vehicle, I began to tell them about Jesus. There at the roadside, at the very entrance to the town, they sat one by one with their feet in the bowl as they surrendered their lives to Jesus. After giving them each a Bible, I walked away choked with emotion as I realised God's faithfulness had so swiftly been demonstrated, despite the negativity of those people who had maintained, 'Folk will never let you wash their feet in this town.' I realised once again that as I had kept my eyes on Jesus, the unexpected had come to pass.

Often out on the road you don't know what is waiting for you literally around the next corner. Another such unexpected moment, also involving a breakdown, occurred one winter's morning, as I was winding my way through a cutting in the Ngabeni Reserve, situated between Port Shepstone and Harding in Southern Natal.

I was accompanied by a farmer friend of mine, Bruce, who was explaining to me the inner struggle he was having, simply walking with me out on the road that day. So often as Christians, our good intention is to be a witness for Jesus, but somehow when it comes to being that, especially in an area where we are well-known, or with our friends or colleagues, we find that the lie of the enemy puts us under condemnation. As a result we tend to shrink back, causing the Lord to have no pleasure in us.

Bruce comes from a well-known farming family in that area and as he was explaining the challenges of walking with me, I noted that he kept his hat pulled well down over his eyes, lest any of the other farmers in the community notice him. As we rounded a corner, we came upon a broken-down Baker's biscuit truck. As we approached, I could see the Indian driver and his assistant waiting patiently behind the vehicle. I must confess that the evangelist in me leapt for joy as I realised that a truck fully laden with biscuits provided a powerful incentive for the driver and his assistant to stay put. Hallelujah, I thought, we have a captive audience. Bruce and I introduced ourselves and began to chat about the love of Jesus. It emerged that the driver was a Hindu who had never had the gospel of Jesus explained to him. The more we talked the more evident it became that there was much anger and bitterness in this man's life.

Sensing his hidden hurts, we began to tell him about Jesus, and shared the gospel with him in a way that he had never experienced before. He then began to open his heart to us, telling us that when he was five years old, he had witnessed his mother being hacked to death with a panga by some primitive tribesmen. He too had been attacked and four finger stubs bore mute testimony, all these years later, to the savagery of the onslaught. Taking his shirt off, he showed us deep gashes in his back also inflicted during that same horrific incident. As he sat with his feet in the bowl he told us that he had never seen this kind of love: a love that would come to

him and show him unconditional compassion and
acceptance. With conviction he said that if this Jesus
could come and wash his feet in spite of all that he had
ever held in his heart, he wanted to live the rest of his
life serving this Saviour who had died for him. As he
sat by his broken truck at the roadside, working through
the strong emotions that had surfaced in so short a time,
his assistant stood looking on, and when we had
finished, declared that he also wanted to serve the King
of kings and the Lord of lords. Then he too sat at the
roadside and we had the privilege of showing him the
servant-love of Jesus as he was born into a glorious
kingdom that cannot be shaken.

Praise God that he is the God of all creativity, but yet
the God of the unexpected. Sometimes it is precisely
when God has been adjusting our characters and we
have repented that he once again brings the unexpected
upon us, just to see how well we have learned
the lesson. One morning, while praying, I found
myself complaining to God: 'Lord, where are all the
opportunities out here?' Now, I don't know why I was
complaining because hardly a day goes by out on
the road without something special taking place.
Nevertheless, as I continued in this vein, the Lord
suddenly began to rebuke me.

Ninety per cent of the time I find that God speaks to
me through his word, and this occasion was no
exception. I was prompted to turn to Isaiah 42:18,
and read,

Hear, you deaf! And look, you blind, that you may see. Who
is blind but My servant, or so deaf as My messenger whom
I send? Who is so blind as he that is at peace with Me, or
so blind as the servant of the Lord? You have seen many
things, but you do not observe them; Your ears are open
but none hears.

I sensed the Lord saying, 'David, you are my servant
whom I send, yet you are so blind and so deaf that you
are even at peace with me.' It was almost like the old

adage: 'Ignorance is bliss'. At first I couldn't quite understand what the Lord was driving at, but when I enquired, I felt the Lord saying, 'You ask where all the opportunities are, but what about the young man you met at the telephone booth the other day?' I said, 'I'm sorry, Lord. I repent of not witnessing to him.' He asked again, 'What about the old lady you helped across the street last week?' I replied, 'Yes, Lord, I know, but I never shared your love.' He asked again, 'What about the lady you chatted to in the shop the other day?' Again I replied, 'I'm sorry, Lord.'

I began to cry out to God and to ask forgiveness for being so insensitive to all the divine opportunities that I had missed, in just the past week. But God is a gracious Father. As we faithfully repent, he faithfully forgives us and not only forgives us but restores us perpetually. As I was repenting my eyes fell on verse 16 of the chapter that I had just read, and immediately sensed the grace of God being extended towards me.

> And I will lead the blind [I realised that was me] by a way that they do not know; in paths they do not know I will guide them. I will make darkness into light before them and rugged places into plains. These are the things I will do, and I will not leave them undone.

I could feel God's grace flooding me and restoring me. I had a deep sense that God had once again dealt with me, that the Spirit had wooed me to repentance and that I had been moulded and honed a little more to reflect the beauty of my Creator. Little did I realise at the time, however, that the Lord was shortly about to check whether I had learned my lesson. That afternoon while out on the road, feeling alert in the Spirit, knowing that my spiritual blindness and deafness had been dealt with, I did what I usually do while out on the road in the country. I asked, 'Lord, what is going on out here today?'

Not long after this, I noticed a highway patrol car drive past me, slow down in the distance, make a U-turn and start driving back towards me. As the car approached

me, it moved off the tarmac onto the gravel at the side
of the road where I was walking, and pulled up right in
front of me. 'Oh no, Lord, I don't need trouble today,'
I thought as I watched a huge provincial traffic officer
unfold himself from the car and walk ominously towards
me. Peering down at me, he enquired, 'What are you
doing?'

'I am walking to Cape Town,' I replied, which made
him look at me rather strangely, as I was going in almost
the opposite direction. I went on to tell him about Jesus
and how my love for him had compelled me to walk
across the Southern continent, showing his servant-love
to all whom I met. At this he became even more puzzled
and I could see that he really didn't understand what I
was sharing with him. But he decided that he liked me
anyway, and not only that, but he was going to adopt
me. Thereupon, he turned his highway patrol car around
and proudly announced that he would escort me to the
next town.

So there I was walking along with cross, bowl and
the whole paraphernalia that accompanies my road
ministry, being escorted on the opposite side of the road
by a highway patrol car with the blue light flashing and
the provincial traffic officer hanging out of the window.
In between the traffic passing I was telling him about
Jesus. Inwardly, however, I was still asking the Lord,
'Lord, what is going on out here today?' We hadn't gone
very far when his car began to overheat through driving
so slowly, and I suggested to him that he go and wait
at the crest of a hill which we could see in the distance.
He protested in Afrikaans, 'Nee, ek ry saam met jou,'
which translated means, 'No, I am riding with you!' We
hadn't got much further, when a motorist passing in his
small bakkie (pick-up truck) suddenly jammed on his
brakes, pulled over and jumped out. It turned out the
man was a Christian and he enthusiastically began
to exchange stories with me, while the cop was still
looking curiously on. Just before the man departed he
clapped hands on me and prayed for me, then pulled

two ten-rand notes out of his pocket, thrust them into my hand and went on his way. I turned to the cop, whose lower jaw by this stage was hanging well clear of his upper one.

I stepped across the road and said to him, 'Isn't God good?'

'*Ja*,' (yeah) he replied.

'Look,' I said, 'the Lord wants to bless you with ten rand.'

'*Ek kan nie jou geld neem nie*,' (I can't take your money) he protested, but I went on to assure him that God wanted to bless him, and so he eventually reluctantly took the ten rand. I simply felt that God wanted me to witness to him and show him that as we freely receive, so we are freely to give. As we proceeded on our way, in spite of God's dealings with me that very morning, I again enquired, 'Lord, what's going on out here today?' still not realising what spiritual blindness and deafness I was continuing to walk in.

As darkness began to close in on us, the cop decided that he would pull his bureaucratic rank on me and started to insist that if I did not get into his car and ride with him, I would get knocked down by the passing traffic. I took great pains to explain to him that the Lord had told me to walk and that I was not to receive a lift from anyone. So into the evening I continued with the blue light flashing, piercing the darkness, as he patiently and faithfully escorted me until we reached the outskirts of the town in which we had the caravan parked. At the border of the town, I finally consented to allow him to load me up, so with his light flashing and siren wailing, my new-found friend delightedly hurtled us on two wheels round corners as he took me Hollywood car-chase style back to the caravan. And as I hung on in the patrol car I was still asking, 'Lord, what's going on out here today?'

My wife's expression as we arrived with a screech of tyres was a sight to behold. She thought I had been arrested. It was only then, however, that God revealed what had been going on all day, once more extending grace even though I had again been insensitive to his Spirit. We invited the traffic officer into the caravan, and shared the message of the redeeming love of Jesus with him. He went quiet as he sat pensively and listened, beginning to realise the price that Jesus had paid for him on the cross. Finally, he sat outside our caravan door with his feet in the bowl, now almost like a little boy despite his uniform which in other circumstances could have been somewhat intimidating. Quietly, he received Jesus into his life as his Lord and Saviour. He went on to tell us how he had been trapped by a spirit of alcoholism and we then cast it out of him in the name of Jesus. As he left, we stood and watched him drive off into the distance, rejoicing in the full knowledge of the freedom of his new-found Saviour.

Unbeknown to us this story was to have a beautiful sequel almost two years later and nearly 2,000 kilometres away from the town in which it had taken place. It occurred as I was winding my way out of the lovely Southern Cape town of George, headed towards Mossel Bay. It was a mild sunny winter's morning and I was on the final leg of the beautiful Garden Route, through which I had been walking for several weeks. All of a sudden, a car pulled up next to me. Glancing across to my right, I noted the red stripes, blue star on the door and blue light on the roof that marked this as a Cape provincial highway patrol car. The driver leaned out and said, 'You don't remember me?' My heart leapt for joy as I hastily replied, 'Of course I do! Your name is Danie; you are world-famous. I have told people about you in different parts of the world.' With that he leapt from the car, ran across the road, and we hugged each other, enthusiastically enjoying this happy reunion. My first question to him was, 'Are you still walking with Jesus?'

His reply was totally affirmative, and he eagerly told me about the Lord's dealings with him since that time. He then asked if I remembered casting the spirit of alcoholism out of him. He went on to tell me that he was totally free and that God had indeed delivered him. At that moment my heart almost burst with joy, because so often in the ministry one is not sure whether a planted seed takes root. 'Are you a member of a church?' I asked, and as God would have it, he was involved in the very church that I was due to preach at in Mossel Bay the following night. He said that he was on duty then but would swop shifts with a colleague so that he and his wife could be at the service.

The next night, as I entered the church, I could see Danie and his wife sitting in the packed congregation. This posed an acid test for me personally. I am only too aware of the lack of credibility that the body of Christ can face when testimonies and so-called miracles are found to be untrue. I have always asked Carol to hold me strictly accountable while preaching and giving accounts of God's dealings with us out on the road. I had shared the story of this traffic officer in many different towns and churches in South Africa as well as abroad. Now here tonight was the opportunity for him to hear his own story and to check its validity.

I decided to tell the story exactly as I had always told it, with all its graphic detail and humour. As the story unfolded, the congregation roared with laughter, none of them in the least suspecting that the main character in the story was sitting right in their midst. As I shared point after point, I could see Danie and his wife, rocking with laughter and clapping, Danie nodding his head in acknowledgement as with a broad grin on his face, he seemed to be spurring me on. When I got to the part where he surrendered his life to the Lord, and the spirit of alcoholism was cast out of him, the congregation was visibly moved. Then I leaned forward and said, 'He is with us tonight; he is right here in your midst. His name is Danie, and he's sitting over there.' The congregation erupted as they clapped and gave thanks to the Lord, while I rejoiced in God's faithfulness.

This incident once again reminded me that God is the God of the unexpected, that his faithfulness is ever-creative. The unexpected can be delightful, rewarding and have eternal results—if we choose to see what the Lord intends us to see. We can either see the waves or we can see Jesus. We can either step out of the boat and say, 'Lord, here I come,' or we can scream, 'Help, it's a ghost!'

8

Sending out the Seventy

It was a swelteringly hot summer's day as I wound my way up an extremely steep mountain pass in the Ciskei, a small 'independent homeland' in the Eastern Cape. Apart from the intense heat and the perspiration pouring down my body from the climb, I was thoroughly enjoying life. Spotting a tiny thorn tree over to my right, I decided that any shade would be better than none, and shedding my water tanks and foot-washing gear, I crawled in under the little shade that the thorn bush afforded.

I was lying there, relaxing and feeling that I was born for such a time as this, when in the distance I heard a strange sound. Trying to convince myself that it was definitely not the sound I feared, I popped my head ostrich-like out beyond the thorn tree to check. Much to my horror my suspicions proved true. The faint distant boom, boom I was hearing was the warlike beating of tribal drums. A large crowd of Xhosa tribesmen was headed towards me, fully clad in all their tribal regalia and weaponry, spoiling for a faction fight. My heart almost stopped beating even as my mind started racing. There was no human being that I could call on for help, and there was no way that I could run for it as that would almost certainly have provoked a chase. To say I felt scared would be a gross understatement. Muttering to myself, 'If this is my day to graduate to heaven, I might as well graduate on my feet,' I hastily donned my contraption and picked up the cross and bowl. Like a flash the remembrance of what God had taught me early on in my days out on the road came back to me: the word of God never retreats and the cross always goes forward.

My hands were sweating so profusely from sheer terror that I could hardly hold the cross and bowl as I started to walk towards the armed warriors. As I took each step, I was praying fervently in the Spirit. No lukewarm prayer could hold back what was coming towards me now. I realised that to this chanting, jogging, action-hungry group of warring men, a lone white man was a tempting target. I could now see them clearly, fifty metres away, then forty metres, thirty metres, twenty metres. In a split second they would be on top of me.

Suddenly I did something without knowing why. In a flash, I raised the cross and bowl high above my head and shouted the words, 'Uyesu uyinkosi'—the only Xhosa words I had ever learned—meaning 'Jesus is King'. Instantly every one of them stopped dead in his tracks as though his feet had been cast in concrete.

The silence was deafening. You could have heard the proverbial pin drop. Then like a general examining the ranks, I started moving through them, placing fluorescent green 'I'm walking with Jesus' stickers on each of their bare chests. As I reached the other end of the group they nodded as one man, and immediately bounded on their way, chanting, their shields and assegaais (spears) waving as they went to slaughter their enemy, plastered with Jesus stickers. I just stood and shook my head in amazement as I saw them disappear into the distance, knowing once again that God's faithful hand is able to deliver us out of every trial.

People often ask what I do when I am walking out in the country, particularly in lonely places where it is very quiet. 'Why don't you read a book,' they suggest, 'or listen to a Walkman?' The advice is always well-meant, but how can I really explain to them the dynamics of what takes place out on the road?

For one thing, there are always physical pressures.

Carrying a twenty-plus kg (45lb) load day in, day out, in blistering heat, torrential rain or bone-chilling cold, and covering up to thirty kilometres per day on foot is always tiring, no matter how fit you are. I move the cross and bowl from hand to hand, but even so it feels like a ton weight by day's end.

Perhaps even more testing to one's endurance are the pressures from the unseen realm. I have come to know that every time I set foot on the road, the powers of hell are mobilised against me. Often the warfare in the Spirit is intense, a battle without let-up, demanding total concentration. Then there are, too, the ever-present dangers of mugging, of being misled by deceivers and chancers, not to mention the very obvious hazards of walking thousands of kilometres right on the edge of high speed traffic.

To counteract all this I constantly praise the Lord. I sing a lot and pray perpetually under the power of the Holy Spirit, asking him to give me discernment and show me what he would have me do each step of the way. As I do this, the Lord reveals time and again in the Spirit what I am to do, and I attempt to be obedient to what the Spirit shows me.

Walking and praying in this fashion one day as I trudged on through the Ciskei, I realised I was passing the elite Fish River Sun gambling casino and resort. I started praying in the Spirit, sensing the prevailing stronghold that was over this magnificent spot. There was a cry from within my spirit, saying, 'Lord, wouldn't it be beautiful if you could touch the very heart of this place?' As I strolled past I did not feel that the Spirit was saying, 'Go in,' but I continued to intercede, just waging spiritual warfare and trusting that God would in some way place his finger on what I had been praying into.

That day Carol had been doing what we call 'leap-frogging'. She drives the car and caravan past me, stopping some kilometres down the road. As I pass her, she allows me to go some distance and then passes me again. When she picked me up that evening and we

headed off to the spot where we were spending the night
in our caravan, I shared with her what my cry for the
Fish River Sun had been. As we prayed that night, we
had a clear impression from the Holy Spirit that I needed
to be out on the road early the next morning, far earlier
than I would be normally. In obedience to that word, I
rose early the next day, not knowing why but trusting
the Lord that he indeed had brought me out at this time
for some special purpose. I had not travelled for long,
when I came to a small sand-road intersection outside
a little settlement. At the precise moment I reached the
intersection, a small *bakkie* (pick-up truck) drew up in
front of me. The driver recognised me, greeted me
warmly and asked if I would come to his house for a
cup of coffee. At this point I almost missed the Holy
Spirit, thinking that he had brought me out on the road
and that I had better be faithful and remain there.

Suddenly I felt the quiet prompting of the Spirit saying
to me, 'Go with him.' I thanked the driver for his offer,
placed the cross and bowl on the back of his *bakkie* and
headed off to his house. On the way he explained to me
that he and his wife were both Christians and that they
truly loved the Lord. On our arrival, his wife emerged,
recognised me and greeted me with much joy and
excitement. She then introduced me to a friend standing
alongside her who had arrived just minutes earlier
through some misunderstanding. I greeted her friend
and felt prompted to ask her, 'Do you love Jesus?' She
stammered, back-pedalled and said, 'N-n-no, not like
these people.' I immediately said to her, 'I believe you
will meet Jesus today.'

We all had a good chat over coffee and I shared with
them some of the experiences I had had along the
roadside. Finally, I turned to the friend of my hostess,
a lady in her early thirties. We started to talk about Jesus
and I explained what Jesus had done for her on the cross,
how man's sin separates him from God, and that Jesus
said, 'Unless a man is born again, he cannot see the
Kingdom of God' (Jn 3:3).

We chatted for some time and occasionally the lady would ask questions and even raise objections. Eventually, she surrendered her life to the Lord as I washed her feet. Her friends were elated, particularly the lady of the house, who hugged her with great joy. I was deeply grateful that God in his faithfulness had allowed me the opportunity so early that morning to see his work, yet I still had not realised the full implication of what had just happened. Once the ministry was complete, I reloaded the cross and bowl on the *bakkie* and we headed back towards the main road. It was only then that I was to learn precisely what God had just done. As we went bumping along the man asked, 'Do you know who that woman was?'

'No.'

'She's the wife of the general manager of the Fish River Sun.'

Alone on the highway once more, my prayer was one of overwhelming gratitude as I said, 'God, thank you for allowing me to be your humble servant.' With a bounce in my step, I went on my way singing, 'Here I am, wholly available.'

My time of moving from the Ciskei towards Port Elizabeth was truly a joyful time as we went from one meeting to another in the small town of Grahamstown, then pushed on through Bushman's River and the small village of Alexandria, where my mother had been born over seven decades before. I recalled how my grandmother used to keep us enthralled with stories of how, as a little girl, she would go by horse and buggy from Alexandria to Sand Flats, taking a couple of days. She told us delightful stories about a character called Oom Paul Feck and his misdemeanours, most of which I would be too embarrassed to relate here. Once again it was lovely to be in this quaint little place and to encounter parts of my roots and heritage. God was faithful near Alexandria and we saw his Spirit poured out upon many as lives changed and people came into the fulness of what God had for them.

Now Port Elizabeth, a large seaport, lay ahead. Its northern access, the route I was walking, is via a rather grimy industrial area populated by its own unique characters. A breed apart, they lead rough tough lives and speak their own particular brand of slang. For example, a friend would be referred to as 'my china'. As I was strolling through this rather unromantic part of what is a very beautiful city, I came eyeball-to-eyeball with one of the locals. Or more accurately, perhaps, he came eyeball-to-eyeball with me. Pedalling up on a large black bicycle with balloon tyres, he ground to a halt in front of me, placing a foot on the pavement to steady himself. His face could best be described as battle-scarred, sporting as it did a deep gash of a scar across his nose. As he peered at me with somewhat bloodshot eyes, I noticed that he had a revolver tucked into his belt.

'Excuse me, my mate, are you new around here?'

I could picture how I must look to him with my cross and bowl, contraption, towels, chair and T-shirt declaring 'Jesus-washed feet are happy feet'.

'Yes, I guess you could say I'm new around here,' I grinned in reply, realising my image didn't exactly fit the environment.

'Well, I just want to warn you that down the road is the New Brighton Station (a black residential area), and if you go there they will strip you of every single thing you have.'

I thought, 'Praise God, that means that I must be in the right place.' Then just as he was about to proceed on his way, I said to him, 'Excuse me, Sir, would you mind if I asked you a question?' He said that he didn't mind.

'Do you love Jesus?' I asked. He reeled back on his saddle, attempted to focus on me and exclaimed emphatically, 'O Jesus, is my favourite china!'

It took all my self-control to keep a straight face as I said farewell to him and went on my way, calling in on the folk at New Brighton Station. To my delight, six men there gave their lives to the Lord, with their feet in the bowl. All men, no women; that just must be God's way of plundering hell in the most difficult of situations. Port Elizabeth was once again to be one of those cities where God gave us the most amazing favour with the city's peoples and the body of Christ. The love and care that we experienced from the believers in this city was unprecedented. They ensured that we had meals brought round to our caravan each evening. Our washing would be collected by a lady from one of the churches each day and be returned ironed the next day. Our caravan was a never-ending hub of activity as people came to bless us, to encourage us, to experience that which Jesus was doing in our lives, to find salvation. Others would bring their burdens in an attempt to have their needs met by the power of the Holy Spirit.

As in all cities, I once again started to wait on the Lord to see if there was anything he wanted to do in this beautiful city. Day after day I would get alone in some quiet spot on a lonely beach and wait for many hours upon the Lord as, waging war in the Spirit, I attempted to see what God would do in this lovely place. The answer was a long time coming, but bit by bit God showed me what it was to be. It started in the book of Acts, as I began to read and re-read this verse:

And everyone kept feeling a sense of awe, and many wonders and signs were taking place through the apostles. And all those who had believed were together, and had all things in common; and they began selling their property and possessions, and were sharing them with all as anyone might have need (Acts 2:43–45).

As I thought about these verses, I was particularly touched by the words, 'everyone kept feeling a sense of awe', 'had all things in common' and that there wasn't a needy one among them. I couldn't help saying to the Lord, 'Lord, wouldn't it be beautiful if that could be said of your church here in Port Elizabeth?' For days and days I came back to this passage, feeling a deep sense of excitement over it, knowing that the Spirit was stirring something within me. After some days, I sensed the

Lord saying, 'Yes, David, that can be here in Port Elizabeth.'

Obviously my next question was, 'How will you bring this to pass, Lord?' As I began to wait, I clearly sensed the Lord once again saying to me, 'See what I did and do what I did.' I had heard those words before and so knew exactly what to do: go back to the Gospels to see what Jesus had done. I found myself in Luke's Gospel, where Jesus was instructing the seventy, sending them out

two and two ahead of Him to every city and place where He Himself was going to come. And He was saying to them, 'The harvest is plentiful, but the labourers are few; therefore beseech the Lord of the harvest to send out labourers into His harvest. Go your ways; behold, I send you out as lambs in the midst of wolves' (Lk 10:1–3).

I went on to read (v 16): 'The one who listens to you listens to Me, and the one who rejects you rejects Me, and he who rejects Me rejects the One who sent Me.'

Luke's Gospel continues: 'And the seventy returned with joy, saying, "Lord even the demons are subject to us in Your name." And He said to them, "I was watching Satan fall from heaven like lightning"' (vv 17–18).

[Jesus continued] 'Nevertheless do not rejoice in this, that the spirits are subject to you, but rejoice that your names are recorded in heaven.' At that very time He rejoiced greatly in the Holy Spirit and said 'I praise Thee, O Father, Lord of Heaven and earth, that Thou didst hide these things from the wise and intelligent and didst reveal them to babes. Yes, Father, for thus it was well pleasing in Thy sight' (vv 20–21).

And turning to the disciples, He said privately 'Blessed are the eyes which see the things you see, for I say to you, that many prophets and kings wished to see the things which you see and did not see them, and to hear the things which you hear, and did not hear them' (vv 23–24).

That was it! The Lord was saying that the church would meet the needs of those in the city of Port Elizabeth as we sent out the seventy. He promised that those who listened to the people we sent would be listening to Jesus and the one who sent Jesus. He promised to rejoice with us as we returned. He promised that we would see Satan fall from heaven like lightning and assured us that even prophets and kings would wish to see and hear the things that we were to witness, but that they would not. What a privilege! I was so excited and filled with expectancy that I could hardly contain what God was confirming to me. However, I have learnt never to rush in, but to be sure that it is God who is speaking. At this point, I had to fly up to Johannesburg for two days to fulfil an engagement, and having returned to the caravan was wearily lying in my bunk that night, saying, 'Lord, it's now time to move on or to implement what you have shown. Please, I ask you to confirm one of them urgently.'

I am a firm believer in not scratching around in the Scriptures trying to find a verse that fits what you believe God is saying to you. More often than not God will speak from the very place where you are reading at that time. For the past few days, I had been reading the Epistle of James, and having just prayed asking God to give me confirmation, that night I started reading these words,

> What use is it, my brethren, if a man says he has faith, but he has no works? Can that faith save him? If a brother or sister is without clothing and in need of daily food, and one of you says to them, 'Go in peace, be warmed and filled,' and yet you do not give them what is necessary for their body, what use is that? Even so, faith, if it has no works, is dead, being by itself (Jas 2:14–17).

If the Lord had spoken to me audibly it could not have been more clear. I was to go ahead with the sending out of the seventy. As I continued to wait on the Lord in prayer, I felt that we were to gather at the main King's Beach each night for four nights and then send out the seventy, two by two. Each one was to have two prayer partners who would undertake to pray as they were out ministering to the poor and needy. On their return those who had gone out would meet with their prayer partners and report back on the needs discovered that night. And then on the final night we were to rejoice by holding a celebration time of worship and witnessing, just as Jesus would have done as the seventy returned. Unfortunately, the timing of what was to happen was rather awkward for most churches as it was Holy Week, the week leading up to the Easter weekend. This, however, did allow me the opportunity to share in many situations and with a cross-section of the church leadership within the city. I felt I should have seven people from each of ten different churches, as it was the desire of my heart for this thing not to be owned by *a* church but *the* church.

The first evening as we assembled, the wind was blowing with an intensity that only Port Elizabethans know. I had spent the past few days moving through the poorer and more needy areas of the city in an attempt to determine exactly which streets the seventy should visit in the different parts of the city. I instructed the seventy that they did not go as representatives of any church, but were merely to knock on the doors of houses and say, 'Good evening, we have come to serve you as the Christians of the city of Port Elizabeth.' They were then to enquire whether there were any needs in that home, physical, spiritual or simply a prayer need.

My wife Carol had been prompted to cook a few meals which we took with us, and as we knocked on doors, we would present the people with a meal, simply to bless them, often much to their astonishment. We never went with any hidden agenda, purely to love people in the name of Jesus and to meet their needs. On the first night, however, as we visited one family, we found that without our trying to evangelise them, they surrendered their lives to Jesus. We then went on calling on other homes, accompanied by Paula, a young friend of ours.

Each evening we returned to those homes and in one home we visited, only on the third night did I say to the lady, 'I would like to talk to you about Jesus.' Her reply was, 'I wondered when you were going to talk about Jesus.' Their hearts were so open that she and her husband plus a friend present immediately surrendered their lives to the Lord. Later, we discovered that they had already filed papers for divorce. In the ensuing days, the divorce application was withdrawn, a testimony to Jesus making all things new. In the weeks ahead another family was integrated into one of the local churches, becoming new creations, as old things passed away and new things came.

On the first night, as we returned to King's Beach, we were greeted with a buzz of excitement as the seventy gathered, many of them with their prayer partners. People would call out the needs they had uncovered, while someone else in the crowd would offer to help meet the need. Some of the requests were so extreme, I couldn't help wondering what would happen the next night as we once again gathered to send out the seventy.

The following evening as we met, my heart leapt for joy at the unbelievable sight that met my eyes down at King's Beach. There were piles of food, clothing, men's suits. There was an electric geyser, a bed, tins of paint and paint-brushes, ready-cooked meals and much more that the seventy brought and laid at the feet of the church leaders of the different denominations. Truly this was the Acts church in action once again. 'For there was not a needy person among them, for all . . . would . . . bring the proceeds of the sales, and lay them at the apostles' feet; and they would be distributed to each, as any had need' (Acts 4:34–35). The seventy then headed out to go and perform their work, breaking bondages and setting captives free from both spiritual and physical chains. This glorious process continued night after night; everyone felt a sense of awe and many signs and wonders were taking place, just as God had prophesied.

Little did we know that on the final night, we were to see God fulfil his promise with pinpoint accuracy as we celebrated with joy the return of the seventy. The city authorities had graciously granted us permission to hold the celebration in the open air at Happy Valley, but as that final day progressed, the wind and the elements rose up and became more and more intense. At four o'clock in the afternoon we realised that there was no way that the meeting could go on in the open and so took the decision with the gracious consent of Ivan Vorster, senior pastor of the large Harvest Church, to move the celebration to their lovely building. We placed one or two volunteers in Happy Valley to redirect people to the Harvest Church.

I had imagined that we would have just a small group comprising the seventy with their prayer partners, although we had encouraged them if possible to bring any converts they had had throughout the week. We also arranged for a composite worship team to lead worship for the evening to ensure that it truly was a time of high celebration as the seventy returned. Much to my amazement, the Harvest Church was almost packed with several hundred people and there was great expectancy as the time of celebration got off with a bang. Songs of worship were interspersed with testimony to God's faithfulness: how we had seen children kitted out with brand new school uniforms, houses painted, people given furniture. We had even taken an offering at one stage to pay a rather large electricity bill so that a family could have lights and water again. People who had been saved gave testimonies, and then the moment occurred when the Lord was to bring his word to completeness with deadly accuracy.

As I stood on the platform, I saw a church leader at the back of the auditorium with a very large man alongside him. After several songs, the leader beckoned to me indicating that the man wished to share a testimony. I nodded and the man moved towards the platform. As he stepped up I handed him the microphone. After uttering a few words, he aggressively said he did not want to use it and thrust it back at me. He went on to say to the people, 'I am a child of the kingdom of darkness . . .'

'Hallelujah,' I thought, 'this is going to be a good testimony.' However, he continued, 'There is nothing I can do to get out of it and there is nothing that you can do to get me out.' I was horror-struck, realising in an instant that this man was not out of the kingdom of darkness but still in it. Here was Satan at the helm of a Christian meeting. However could I have let this happen? He went on to say that he could have anything he wanted and that he had everything that he had ever desired. 'The only thing,' he said, 'that I cannot have is love.'

At this point my mind was racing, knowing that there was no way we could physically remove him, as he towered above me. Fortunately I had the microphone in my hand and I boomed out across the public address system as I stopped him, saying, 'You *can* get out of this darkness and you *can* get out tonight; Jesus will help you.' I realised that Satan was so stupid that he had attempted to hijack our meeting by walking right into the middle of it. I knew that the Bible said that one would put a thousand to flight, but that two would put ten thousand to flight. How little chance did Satan stand in this Spirit-charged place with all these believers?

I called on six of the pastors and ministers present and asked him to go out with them, deciding that there was no way we would give Satan the pleasure of disrupting the meeting. After the pastors had taken him out, I instructed the people to pray fervently in the Spirit. I did not want anyone praying in English, Afrikaans or other mother tongue, as this was indeed a spiritual battle. They took him to a small prayer room where they counselled and prayed over him as we went on, after battling in the Spirit, to praise and glorify God, rejoicing in all that had taken place in the past days. The pastors continued for several hours with the Satanist, attempting to deliver and counsel him. The spiritual battle was so intense at one stage that the man took off his clothes and started to rip them up each time they attempted to get him to say the name of Jesus. He did however manage to utter the name of Jesus before they departed.

It was only some weeks later as I picked up a national magazine and read how a Port Elizabeth pastor had finally led this man through into salvation, delivered him from the bondages of hell and baptised him in the name of Jesus, that I realised that in that week we had seen every single element fulfilled. We had sent the disciples out two by two as lambs among wolves, we had seen the seventy return with joy, we had witnessed that there wasn't a needy one among them, and finally we had even watched Satan fall from heaven like lightning. I could not help exclaiming, 'Great is thy faithfulness, O Lord.'

9

Simply . . . Servanthood

Her chest heaved and shuddered as she gasped for breath, straining to get air in, struggling to get it out again. As she stared up at me, her eyes were panic-stricken, helpless as a wounded deer, mutely pleading with me to do something. With my hands on her head I cried out, 'Lord, I beg you to heal her, by the blood of Jesus. I plead with you to set her free. Cause your "Son" to rise on her with healing in his wings.' But as I looked down at her she continued to heave red-faced, gasping for breath. It seemed hopeless, and each moment I felt more and more desperate.

The morning meeting in this excellent church had been vibrant and exciting and several had come to salvation. Now with the meeting over and the church mostly emptied, I found myself crying out for this woman gasping for her life with the most extreme asthma attack I have ever witnessed. Moment by moment her condition seemed to deteriorate as I continued to plead with the Lord, with no apparent result. I generally find that when I am praying for the sick, the Lord seems not to act when I pray eloquent, well-organised prayers, but when in moments of desperation, I bombard heaven and cry out, the Holy Spirit honours my prayers. This was one such occasion, but still nothing seemed to be happening. On the contrary, this dear mother of two small children appeared to be slipping further and further away as she continued to gasp for breath and for her life.

At this point, I backed off slightly and quietly said to the Lord, 'Show us what to do.'

I sensed the Lord reply, 'It's the anointing that breaks the yoke.' I did not understand what the Lord was saying. Again I asked the question, and again the reply came, 'It's the anointing that breaks the yoke.' Somewhat puzzled by this reply I continued to pray in the Spirit and eventually said, 'What anointing, Lord?' I then sensed the Holy Spirit ask me the question, 'What are you anointed to do?' I wasn't sure just what to reply for the moment, but continued to pray. Eventually I worked out that the only thing that I was anointed to do was to wash feet, so I promptly asked one of the men standing nearby to go and fetch some water as quickly as he could. It seemed an eternity before he returned, while the lady continued to heave and heave as she fought for breath. 'She will be dead before he gets back,' I thought, but we continued to pray in the Spirit and uphold her. Finally the water arrived. I hurriedly poured it into the bowl, and the moment the woman's feet touched the water, her breathing changed and became totally normal. Carol and those who were with me immediately erupted into joyous dancing and clapping. We realised that the Lord had intervened and that the anointing had broken the yoke of bondage of extreme asthma over this woman that had held her captive since she was a tiny girl.

That evening as we returned to the church to lead the evening service, the woman and her husband were present and she reported that she had gone home and slept peacefully that afternoon without a trace of restricted breathing. More than a year later I had the privilege of returning to the same church to receive the glad news that this woman had been totally healed and set free and had had no sign of an asthma attack from that day on. It is beautiful when God acts and when we as his servants have the privilege of being vessels available to be used to his honour and glory.

Servanthood is not only an honour but a call that God extends to each of us. Yet as I observe much of

Christianity today, I see that people are either wrapped up in the blessings of the Lord and forget servanthood or conversely, are so enveloped in servanthood that they overlook the fact that there is a loving Father who chooses to bless them. In Psalm 103:2, the psalmist declares, 'Bless the Lord, O my soul, and forget none of His benefits.' As we examine the word we see that these benefits are indeed bountiful. Jesus declared in John 15:11 that he came that our joy may be full or complete. In John 14:27, he said, 'My peace I give to you; not as the world gives, do I give to you.' There are so many other marvellous benefits that the word goes on to tell us about, for example, that we have been given all authority in Jesus and that we have the benefit of being separated from the law of sin and death by what Jesus did for us on the cross. Without detracting in any way from these marvellous blessings that the Lord has laid up for us, I believe that, as the Holy Spirit looks on the body of Christ today, he is often grieved by those who focus only on the benefits. By so doing they disqualify themselves from ever understanding that God sees characteristics such as righteousness as prerequisites to claiming his marvellous benefits for our lives.

A case in point occurred one day as I was moving through the streets of a city while carrying the cross and bowl, accompanied by a dear friend. Crossing one of the main streets, I saw out of the corner of my eye a man homing in on me from the other side of the road, effusively waving his arms in greeting.

'Brother Dave,' he exclaimed as he got to me, 'what a joy it is to see you, and to meet you.' As he spoke he continued to shake my hand with a pumping action that resembled the driving wheel of a locomotive.

'Praise the Lord,' he said. 'I have heard about you, wanted to meet you and missed you in the other towns you have been in, but I am glad to meet you at last.'

He continued to praise the Lord and Hallelujah him, launching into an articulate barrage of Scripture

quotations that would have made even a theologian's
head spin. A thickset, nicely built, well turned-out man,
he went on to tell us how even though he was struck
down and persecuted, and in spite of the fact that his
wife had left him, he was standing on God's word
believing for the promise of God's peace.

While this verbal bombardment was under way, I
suddenly felt the Holy Spirit start to speak to me.
Unceremoniously, at the first opportunity to get a word
in edgeways, I looked him straight in the eye and said,
'Sit down, I want to wash your feet.' Praising the Lord
and hallelujahing he sat down, shoes and socks flying
in the air as he prepared to place his feet in the bowl.
As soon as I had finished pouring the water into the
bowl from the water tank attached to my back, I placed
my hand on his head and heard the Holy Spirit say,
'Now tell him.' As I began to pray and prophesy, I was
somewhat astounded myself at what I heard proceeding
from my mouth.

'You have been seeking my peace, my son, but it
escapes you. You have been looking here and there for
solutions to the dilemmas of your life, but they escape
you, but I say to you that until you repent of the sin of
homosexuality that grips you, I cannot give you my
peace. Until you acknowledge the hold this homosexuality has upon you I cannot restore your marriage.
Peace I give you, not as the world gives, do I give to you.'

Suddenly I felt the man shaking beneath my hand. I
opened my eyes and saw tears rolling down his cheeks
and his hands raised in the air. He cried out and said,
'God you know that the word which has come from
Dave is true. Please forgive me, Father; I repent. Help
me to walk the straight path in Jesus' name.' I continued
to pray for him as I washed his feet and dried them,
claiming God's protecting hand as he faithfully repented.

Here was a typical case of a man who was striving for
the benefits of God, yet not wanting to fulfil God's
condition of righteousness and holiness. He was an
example of so many Christians who choose to ignore

the sin in their lives and therefore continually fail to walk
in the fulness of the benefit of God's peace. Yet there is
such a rich reward when we walk in righteousness and
holiness and are able to claim the benefits that God in
his marvellous provision, in the power of his Spirit, has
placed within us. Take for example the benefit of the
authority of the believer. In Matthew 28:18 as well as
Luke 9:1, we see how Jesus has given us *all* authority.
We go on to read in 1 Corinthians 15 that God has placed
all things in subjection beneath Jesus' feet and this
includes foreign gods. The word tells us that God is a
jealous God and he will have no other gods before him,
yet so often as Christians we are too scared to confront
others regarding this matter.

One morning while in Natal, which has a considerable
Indian population, I was moving around the carpark of
a large shopping mall. It was a lovely, warm, typically
subtropical, Natal morning. In a relaxed fashion, I was
chatting to the shoppers as they went to and from their
cars, sharing the love of Jesus with them and telling
them about his dealings in my life. Towards the latter
part of the morning, I found myself talking to an Indian
couple accompanied by their teenage son. As I began to
tell the man about Jesus, he said, 'Speak to my wife;
don't speak to me; I am a Hindu.' I smiled politely and
continued to tell him about Jesus. Once again as the
conversation deepened, he said to me, 'Don't speak to
me; speak to my wife; I am a Hindu,' whereupon I
politely continued to smile at him and tell him about
Jesus. Some half an hour later, he sat with his feet in
the bowl in the carpark, hands raised and cried out,
'Jesus, I should have done this long ago,' as he received
Jesus into his life.

The next morning, I was scheduled to preach at a joint
celebration of five churches in the Durban area. I invited
the Indian man, his wife and son to attend the service,
and just before I stood up to preach I called him forward,
not wishing to embarrass him but wanting to encourage
the believers. I started by saying, 'Yesterday this man

served a foreign god; today he serves the only true God and the King of kings and Lord of lords.' As believers we need to claim the benefit of the authority of God and allow ourselves to be consumed by it and use it to his honour and glory.

One might ask, 'All these benefits; what's the price?' Well there is a price, but it has been paid on the cross. Paid in full and there is nothing that we can do to earn or deserve this. It is our *inheritance*. For example, one might look at Prince Charles, who is destined, as the heir to the throne of Great Britain, to inherit kingship, royalty, wealth, and all the authority that comes with the role of king of the United Kingdom. There is nothing that he has to do to earn or even deserve this. Quite simply, it is his inheritance. Now if we are to claim our inheritance or heirship as joint heirs, as members of God's family (Rom 8:17), we are charged with the *stewardship* of preserving the family heritage. *Heirship is responsibility* and in that responsibility Jesus laid down certain conditions. These I believe are focused on the central theme of his life and lifestyle which is that of servanthood.

The first condition that Jesus presented to us was that we were to lay down our lives (Jn 15:13), and yet so many Christians find it difficult even to lay down a little bit of time which might affect their favourite Saturday afternoon TV sports programme.

Secondly, Jesus went on to set the condition that we were to deny ourselves and take up our cross and follow him (Mt 16:24). Sadly most Christians today don't even know what their cross is and are not even aware of what Christ has called them to do or to carry. Obviously, I don't believe that Jesus is telling us all physically to take up a cross and carry it, but as businessmen or professional people we could find that special tool that God would give us to reach the people in our workplaces.

Condition number three: the Bible instructs us in Revelation 3:16 to be red hot and not lukewarm. 'Because you are lukewarm, and neither hot nor cold, I will spit you out of My mouth.' Today within the body of Christ there are many who live in the comforts of 'nice' Christianity. They work with colleagues year in and year out who don't even know where they stand with Jesus. Jesus, however, has clearly told us not to light our lamp and hide it under a bushel.

Fourthly, Jesus instructed us in this specific sense to be servants. 'But it is not so among you, but whoever wishes to become great among you shall be your servant' (Mk 10:43). Not only did Jesus make this statement verbally but his very lifestyle declared it. He washed the disciples' feet, served tens of thousands of people during his time here on earth, went out of his way to raise Lazarus from the dead, cooked breakfast for the disciples after a weary night's toil out on the water, dared to touch the unclean leper and . . . and. . . . The list goes on and on. It is in this area that I believe God has called me to make a prophetic statement of his servant love, and yet it is in this very thing that I find God challenges me harder and more than any other.

One winter's morning I was walking through the beautiful sugar-cane fields of Natal, accompanied by a young man from Iceland, and as we journeyed a stooped figure came into view in the distance. As he drew closer he appeared to be an elderly peasant, leaning heavily with both hands on a tall stick as he hobbled along. That morning, my day had begun in somewhat disorganised fashion as the car had gone in for repairs, and a local pastor's wife had unexpectedly arrived to pick me up and take me out on the road. For the first time ever, in my scurry to gather all my gear together, I had headed out leaving my towels behind.

As we drew nearer to this shuffling figure, we crossed the road to talk to the old man, only to discover he wasn't elderly, but a Zulu man in his late thirties to early forties. Puzzled at why he had been shuffling along so laboriously, we glanced at his feet only to see the most tragic, bloodstained, rotten, leprous limbs imaginable. In a mixture of English with the odd Zulu word, we

managed to ask him where he was headed and he replied
in Zulu that he was going to Murchison. We knew that
there was a mission hospital there but also knew that it
was about an eight kilometre walk from where we were.
The road surface was incredibly rough and for these
rotten, bleeding feet it must have felt like much further.
The man managed to explain to us that the minibus fare
was two rand and that he did not have it. I normally do
not carry money on me when I am out on the road for
many different reasons, but I plunged my hand into my
pocket and there, to my surprise, was the exact amount.
I thrust it into his hand and turned to move on, feeling
there was no way that I could minister to him any further
as I did not have my towels with me.

We bade him farewell and headed on our way. I hadn't
gone more than about ten paces when I heard a small
voice within me say, 'You've grieved me: you never
washed his feet. You never showed him my servant
love.' Hurriedly I scampered back after the man, calling
and beckoning to him. I quickly put the bowl and cross
down on the ground, opened the tap of my water tank
and began to fill the bowl, while seating him on my little
chair. As I did so, I could feel the bite of the chilly winter
air blowing on my arms and the back of my neck, while
everything seemed to be taking place in slow motion. I
looked up and said to my young Icelandic companion,
'I don't know if we could ever explain to him what
we are about to do, but we will just trust the Holy
Spirit to show him.' I then picked up the bleeding,
broken feet before me and placed them gently in the
bowl, washing them and soothing them. I could feel the
tears welling up in my eyes as I prayed that the Lord
might give him understanding of his comforting serving
love.

As I finished, I cried out to the Lord, 'Lord, we now
have no way to dry his feet,' and I sensed the Holy Spirit
reply, 'Take your shirt off and dry his feet.' I pulled my
T-shirt over my head and began to gently dab his feet
until they were totally dry, the blood-stains and mucus

soaking the fabric as I did so. As we finished, I donned
the cross and bowl and the rest of my gear. After bidding
him goodbye, I walked on with my shirt in my hand,
acutely conscious of the freezing wind which I was to
endure the rest of the day. As I turned into bed that
night, pondering what had taken place, I sensed the
Holy Spirit say to me, 'Flesh and blood will not reveal
this to him but your Father who is in heaven.'

The deepest prayer that Carol and I could ever pray
out on the road is that we might just be Jesus to those
with whom we come into contact. Inadequate as we
might feel at times, we choose to stretch our faith and
go out on a limb so that in some small way we might
reflect his beauty and glory. It is often in the times when
we feel least well-equipped that the Lord places the
extraordinary and the supernatural before us. One such
moment was during the days when the Lord was
pouring out his amazing blessings on the city of East
London. A lady tracked us down to the farm where we
were staying outside the city.

It was just past mid-morning when the young mother
in her early thirties arrived and introduced herself to us
as Janet. She was accompanied by her mother and a
friend, both of whom had apparently come to support
her. Carol and I welcomed them and we began what
initially seemed a somewhat formal conversation. As we
chatted further, however, and the atmosphere began to
relax, Janet told us how for months and months she had
been undergoing chemotherapy for terminal cancer. Our
hearts went out to her as she described how the
specialists had now stated that there was nothing more
that they could do for her and that she was just to stay
at home while her health continued to deteriorate. She
shared with us how she had been put on to limited
working hours and how in her job at the bank she was
working mornings only and sometimes just certain days
of the week.

As her story unfolded we had an insight into the
hopelessness of the situation, and I caught a glimpse of

how Jesus must have felt as he stood outside Lazarus'
tomb and wept. In spite of the onslaught, however,
Janet's expression seemed firm and as she spoke I could
feel the absolute assurance of the faith of the Holy Spirit
rising up within me. I could sense the love of Jesus,
tangible and present in the room. I could feel hope, too,
start to rise, a hope that went far beyond the natural
hopelessness of this situation. Before praying for Janet
I felt I needed to turn to the mother and ask about her
standing with Jesus, and then Janet's friend, both of
whom surrendered their lives to the Lord.

Carol and I then turned to Janet. We filled the bowl
with water and placed her feet in it, simply demonstrat-
ing the servant love of Jesus, praying he would bring
forth his healing balm upon her. That day as they left I
had a great sense that the Holy Spirit had placed his
finger of healing upon this lovely young mother. Each
time during subsequent years as I passed through East
London on various ministry trips I enquired about Janet.
Sometimes I heard odd snippets of news, other times
nothing, but always wondered about the dealings of the
Lord in Janet's situation.

Two years after praying for Janet, I was preaching one
evening in the large Christian Centre Church in
East London. After the service, a man came up and
introduced himself to me as Janet's father. He apologised
for the fact that Janet could not be there that night as
she was sharing her testimony of God's faithfulness at
another church in the city. Still, I wondered, was God's
healing plan complete in her life?

Then another year later, one afternoon my secretary
Meryl received a call from a man who introduced himself
as Janet's husband, saying that she had been to the
doctors, had had final tests and X-rays and had been
given a totally clean bill of health. God had healed her
miraculously. We fell on our knees and thanked the Lord
for the privilege of being his servants, once again not
knowing why he had chosen to work through us.

Sometimes people say to me, 'That's all very well for

you, Dave, but you don't know the people whom I work with' or 'You don't know my family' or 'In our town' or 'our country' or 'our culture, the people will be different.' I have found in my experience that no matter what culture you are in or where you are in the world, people have the same problems with sin, with temptation, with immorality and with ungodly living. And I have found that there is a hunger out there, whether it be in the office or the laboratory, or the university lecture room, the workshop floor, or out on the streets, a hunger to hear the good news of Jesus, no matter how people might pretend that they are not interested. Sometimes to show the servant love of Jesus, we just have to be Jesus right where we are, whether at the bus station, at McDonald's, at the supermarket or at our daily place of work.

One day just after entering a city, I was washing a man's feet next to a parking meter, while another man stood looking on. When I had finished, the other man approached me and said, 'Excuse me, sir, may I ask you a few questions?' My reply was, 'I don't know if I have all the answers, but I'll try to answer them.' While I was chatting to the man, a crowd of between sixty and seventy people began gathering on the pavement. For the next few hours, I simply knelt and told people about Jesus as one by one I washed their feet until I was so exhausted that I could no longer continue. I thanked God for what was happening. It seemed to be almost an impossible miracle that grown men, without my saying one word directly to them, would come up to me and say, 'David, I have been listening to what you have been saying for the last hour. I want to repent and give my life to Jesus.'

This goes to prove that it is only the Holy Spirit who brings people under conviction and to salvation and that all we need to do is be Jesus to those who are lost and trapped in a dying world. It all begins to happen as we show forth the genuine servanthood of Jesus. 'Lord, daily order my steps that I might be transformed into your likeness; imperfect as I am, make me a mirror that reflects your uncompromising love. Covenant-keeper, make me like you.'

10

Presidents and Peasants

It was a cold winter's morning as I knelt at the dusty roadside just outside the city of George in the Southern Cape. A Dutch woman named Rita was accompanying me, carrying my towels, as I washed the feet of a Cape coloured woman while she surrendered her life to Jesus. I couldn't help feeling that this peasant woman would be despised and rejected by many and would seem an outcast of society, but to Jesus she was a princess in the kingdom of the Most High God. As I washed the woman's feet, my heart was overwhelmed by the extremes that Jesus died for when he paid the price on the cross. My mind and emotions raced back to what had happened just the day before and the very pair of feet that had preceded this peasant woman's in the bowl.

I felt a deep sense of awe, for once again I had witnessed God's faithfulness. I recalled how before we had ever started out on the road, he had promised exactly what had taken place the day before, and how as he had worked during the months of preparation within my heart, God had clearly shown Carol and myself that we would touch both the poor and the powerful. I realised that there was not one single thing that he had spoken to us in all that time that had not come to pass.

Suddenly my mind was a kaleidoscope of all that had happened out on the road, centred on this simple wooden bowl carved by a peasant man, a bowl that God was using to touch a nation. My mind raced back to a time on the streets of Pietermaritzburg when the pavement had been so crowded with people that I was forced to kneel in the gutter as I washed a man's feet. As I did so, I felt the slime and slush of all the muck that was running down the gutter trickling across my knees and thought, 'Well, Lord, now I am in the gutter for Jesus.' But there was a deep sense of privilege, knowing that I served the King of kings and the Lord of lords and was making that prophetic statement of his servant love once again.

Further impressions crowded through my mind: the evening while carrying the cross and bowl through the Transkei as a large crowd started to follow me. People would run out of hut after hut to greet me. I felt a bit like a Pied Piper leading this large crowd, and I remembered how people just wanted to touch the cross and the Spirit of Jesus. I thought of the many motorists who had stopped on the roadside and with their feet in the bowl met Jesus, and the crowds on the beaches in East London; so many others who just stood and wept as they realised that God was always faithful to fulfil his word.

Once again my mind went back to the events of the previous day. They had had their beginnings almost two years before as I had stood in front of the Union Buildings in Pretoria, the administrative capital of our nation. The event had marked the beginning of my long journey across the sub-continent and as I looked up towards the President's office, the Lord said to me, 'David, I want you to minister to President P. W. Botha and to wash his feet.' At the same time, however, I felt the Holy Spirit further saying, 'The time is not now, but I will show you when.' So as I had set out across Southern Africa, I had hidden this away in my heart, but constantly held the promise dear that surely God, in his faithfulness, would bring to pass that which he had promised.

Almost two years had passed since God had first spoken the word, and I had walked as far as the picturesque little town of Knysna, situated in the beautiful Garden Route along the Cape coast of South

Africa. In the evening, just before turning into bed, I was lingering with the Lord, and sensed that the Holy Spirit was saying that now was the time that I would meet P. W. Botha and minister to him and wash his feet. I felt an excitement rise up within me, not knowing what lay ahead, but having a sense of assurance that God was, once again, about to do one of those unusual, unexpected things in my life. Saying nothing to Carol, I quietly got into bed. The next morning, as we were rising, Carol suddenly stopped in her tracks and said to me, 'Dave, I don't want to lay this on you, but I have a strong feeling that this is the time that you will be ministering to P. W. Botha.'

I dropped what I was doing and leapt across and kissed her, exclaiming, 'That has to be the Holy Spirit because the Lord told me exactly the same thing as I was getting into bed last night.' I went on to say that it would take a miracle because we didn't know anyone who even distantly knew P. W. Botha, and so God would have to make a way. This started us praying fervently into the situation and within a week of God speaking his word to us, a man whom we didn't know, and who as far as we knew was not a born again believer, had made an appointment for us to meet with this long-time, legendary leader of South Africa.

What had happened was that on the Sunday morning after God had spoken this word to us, I preached in a small church in the town of Knysna. During the service I explained how before I even started out on the road God had spoken to me about ministering to President Botha, and the amazing confirmation that God had given to both Carol and myself just the week before. I went on to ask the church to stand in prayer with us that these things would come to pass and that God would make a way. Unbeknown to me, one of the men in the meeting went the following morning to his office and told a colleague what God had shown Carol and myself. The colleague, as it happened, was an acquaintance of President Botha. Immediately he set about making an appointment for Carol and myself to meet this famous leader at his home in the Wilderness area, some sixty kilometres away.

The appointment was duly made for some ten days ahead, and this plunged us into a time of fervent prayer and waiting on the Lord. I said, 'Lord, you have set up this appointment; now you need to show me what you want me to say to this man.' However, as the days ticked by, nothing seemed to come from the Lord. I could not seem to grasp at all what God was saying. And then the ever-sure word of God cut through once again:

> And you shall even be brought before governors and kings for My sake, as a testimony to them and to the Gentiles. But when they deliver you up, do not become anxious about how or what you will speak; for it shall be given you in that hour what you are to speak. For it is not you who speak, but it is the Spirit of your Father who speaks in you (Mt 10:18–20).

I received this promise of Jesus into my heart, but must confess that on more than one occasion thereafter, I mentioned to the Lord that it would be nice if he could tell me a little in advance what I should say. However, this was not to be.

I think that at times like these, the Lord often checks us out and tests us in our faithfulness to see whether we will try and take over in the situation, or whether we will faithfully stand aside and allow his Spirit to have his way. Throughout my life, I have been a hands-on person. When crisis strikes or something looks urgent, I have usually tended to rush in immediately and try an earthly solution, before turning to God and asking for his help. However, graciously over the years, the Lord has slowly been teaching me first to listen to the voice of his Spirit, to be patient and then to move in the perfect timing of the Spirit. Here once again in this situation with President Botha, the Lord was testing me to see if I would faithfully allow his Spirit to have his way and do his will in his perfect timing. But I still didn't find it easy.

Finally the morning dawned when Carol and I were to meet President Botha and his wife. As I loaded the cross and bowl into the boot of my car, along with the towels, I wondered what might occur and what opportunity God might open up. I still just leaned on the word that, even at this late hour, the Spirit would reveal to me what to say. It was about five to ten in the morning as our car swung off the main road and headed down the little street that was clearly marked 'No Entry—Road Closed—Residents Only'.

As we drew up near the gate of the Botha home, a security policeman equipped with a two-way radio stepped out and stopped us.

'May I help you?'

'I have an appointment to see Mr Botha,' I replied.

He checked our identities then said, 'Would you please park your car over there and follow me.'

Carrying the cross and bowl along with my Bible and towels, we followed the security guard across the well-kept lawn and through the lovely garden towards the front door of the house. A South African flag was flying on the large flagpole in the garden. The home was beautifully furnished and panelled exactly as one would expect a Presidential home to be. The furnishings were antique, and Mr Botha was later to explain to us that most of the ornaments, curios and displays that decorated the furnishings had been presentations and gifts from dignitaries from many parts of the world. The security guard asked us to wait in the lounge, saying that Mr Botha would join us shortly.

The ex-President (as he had by then become) did not keep us waiting long, but appeared within a few moments. Suddenly I was standing face to face with the legend who had ruled South Africa for so long, and who had been at the helm as the country had gone through many deep waters and high moments. I am not much given to nervousness, but realised as I stood with my gaze fixed on this man that I was no longer waiting for this appointment, and trusting that it might happen one day, but that this was the very moment! It had finally come to pass, the time in which I, God's servant, had to speak uncompromisingly that which was upon God's heart. For a few moments I was totally thrown, fumbling for words and not quite sure what to say. If Mr Botha noticed my nervousness and awkwardness, he very courteously did not let on, and in fact did his very best to relax both Carol and myself.

He invited us to sit down in his lovely lounge and very soon we were joined by the former First Lady who had for so many years assumed the role of mother figure to our nation, Mrs Elise Botha. She was affectionately known to the South African public as Tannie Elise, while Mr Botha had always been known simply as 'P. W.'. As we relaxed we were under no illusions that we were in a Presidential-type home as we were waited on hand and foot, enjoying tea served on the finest of china, beautiful savoury tarts and cakes in exquisite variety and seemingly endless quantities. The lady in attendance, who was introduced to us as the long-time faithful servant of the Bothas, having been with them for more than twenty years, was always sharply alert to Mr Botha's every need.

Having got the opening formalities behind us, I started to relax and rapidly discovered that Mr Botha's level of briefing was superb. He knew much about me and could tell me that I had been born in Carla in the Transkei, that my father had been a Methodist minister, that he knew the route that I had walked and that I had been a pastor in Randburg before being called to this footwashing ministry of servanthood. We chatted warmly, enthusiastically swopping stories and experiences of our various callings. Suddenly Mr Botha stopped and looked at me with a twinkle in his eye, as he said, 'You know, David, that you will probably never be awarded the Nobel Peace Prize for what you do.' He continued with a grin, 'I have travelled vastly and extensively, often by varied modes of transport, but one thing I have never done is travel the country the way

Standing with P. W. Botha

you do.' From the way he said it, I gathered that he was extremely grateful he had not needed to do so!

Conversation then swung to his career and we started to reflect how when I had been just a youngster in the army in 1965, he had been Minister of Defence. Our conversation covered a broad spectrum ranging all the way from Moshe Dyan to Nelson Mandela through to Kaiser Matanzima. It was fascinating to hear the stories and to pick up the heartbeat of this remarkable man. There was no doubt that he saw himself as a reformer and felt that many of the major injustices of apartheid had been dismantled in his day. For example, the dreaded pass laws, which had caused so many millions of innocent people to spend extended periods of time in prison, had been scrapped during his term of office. Likewise laws prohibiting people freedom of movement and the right to seek employment in whatever area they chose had also all been done away with under his rule. Indeed much of the reform which South Africa was to see in the years to come, had, in fact, been placed on the drawing board and masterminded during his time. Sadly, he was not to receive the acclaim and credit which would justifiably have been his.

In the midst of this conversation, I felt the Holy Spirit prompting me, and I suddenly began to see before me a battle-scarred, weary man. I reached for my Bible and turned to the book of Isaiah. I began to read, 'Yet those who wait for the Lord, will gain new strength; They will mount up with wings like eagles, they will run and not get tired, they will walk and not become weary' (Is 40:31).

In an instant it was as if the Holy Spirit had come with explosive power into the room. Mr Botha began to bare his soul to us. He started to share the hurts of friendships, the people who had failed him, many of whom were well-known public figures. I found my mind racing as I thought to myself, 'Is this actually me sitting here with this man attempting to work through the hurts, regrets and frustrations of broken relationships?'

I referred him to Paul's first letter to the Corinthians

where it says that love 'does not take into account a
wrong suffered' (1 Cor 13:5). I looked at him and asked,
'Have you forgiven these people, because if you haven't,
Mr Botha, this unforgiveness will eat you like a cancer?'
He pondered a while, and then came the reply, 'Yes,
David, although I am hurting, I have forgiven these
people.' I then sensed the Lord was wanting to bless
him with a refreshing anointing of oil from heaven, and
asked if I might have the privilege of washing his feet.
At this, a servant appeared with one of the most beautiful
large porcelain bowls I have ever seen, plus a very large
towel. I explained that I had my cross and bowl with
me and laid it on the floor before him. He placed his
feet in the bowl and while I washed his feet with water,
the Holy Spirit washed him with the oil of anointing that
comes from on high.

It was a tender and precious moment as I knelt at the
feet of this legendary man. I explained to him that he
had been a servant to so many for so long and that in
turn Jesus desired to wash his feet and bless him with
his servant love. I could hear his dear wife sitting nearby
quietly sobbing as Carol wept and placed her arms gently
around Tanne Elise. We prayed, asking Jesus to touch
and bless and restore his dear child.

Then as I was drying his feet, he suddenly looked up.
His face shone as he looked straight at Carol and said,
'My feet are free.' It was as if the Holy Spirit had lifted
him up and shaken the feet of his spirit, breaking the
shackles that might have remained in his heart. I quietly
moved across the room and began to prophesy a word
over Mrs Botha that I felt God had placed in my heart.
The presence of the Holy Spirit was tangible in the room
as God poured out his anointing. It was as if we had
made a covenant with these two dear people and God
had knit our hearts. I went on to ask about the intimacy
of P. W.'s walk with Jesus and he assured me that there
was no way that he could have ever ruled the nation
without the help and sustaining hand of Jesus.

Suddenly it became evident we had a new added

dimension of friendship, favour and covenant with these people. Mr Botha called in all the security policemen to be introduced and shake us by the hand; then we went to meet his secretary. A new excitement seemed to come upon Mr Botha. God had given us favour with man and we felt like family members as they showed us through their beautiful home. Enthusiastically, they told us how they had altered it, refurnished it and rebuilt it over the years. Then we went out onto the lawn with the Bothas and had our photographs taken with the cross and bowl. Before leaving I felt there was one last thing that the Holy Spirit would have me say to this dear man, as I quoted from Revelation 11:15, 'The kingdom of this world has become the kingdom of our Lord, and of His Christ; and He will reign forever and ever.' I said, 'Mr Botha, you have served the kingdoms of this world well, now God wants you to continue to serve his mighty kingdom.'

He looked at me and thanked me as he and Mrs Botha strolled relaxedly towards our car. In courteous, gentlemanly fashion, he opened the door for Carol, and they waved like old friends as our car rolled away from their stately home. Carol and I knew with deep certainty that we were fulfilling God's destiny. We knew for certain that God had given us unprecedented favour with man as we had found two precious friends. I feel that should God give me a word at any time for this legendary man, the links forged that morning are such that he would be open to receive it.

That day once again, God was fulfilling his promise to us, that indeed we would touch the poor and the powerful as humble servants in the kingdom of the King of kings. Who compares with our God? And the next day as I knelt to wash a peasant woman's feet in that same bowl where the ex-President's had previously been, I continued to rejoice in the faithfulness of God, who is no respecter of persons. Indeed, had not Jesus himself said: 'As you have done it for the least of these, you have done it for Me'?

11

Not Given to Mediocrity

I believe that mediocrity is the enemy of God's best, and that compromise is the enemy of the radical. Mediocre men and compromisers have never changed the world, yet people will try constantly to bring God's best back to the mediocre and to water down the radical to the point of compromise.

Jesus was both a radical and the best that God could produce. Continually, while on earth, he warred against mediocrity and compromise, perpetually being the rock of offence as he trod on the toes of the Pharisees and others, ruthlessly dealing with anything that smacked of mediocrity. We read in 2 Peter 1:3 of 'Him who called us by His own glory and excellence'. We live for one reason alone, as I understand the word of God, and that is to give glory to the Father continually and to reflect the excellence of Jesus by whom he has called us.

From the start, Jesus set an amazing example of excellence in everything he did. At the wedding feast in Cana of Galilee, where he performed his first miracle, he didn't merely turn water into some cheap vinegary wine but into a vintage so excellent it astonished the presiding head waiter. We go on to see that as he fed the five thousand he did not just barely make ends meet, but provided in such abundance that once the vast multitude had completed their feast, twelve baskets of food were left over, proving once again that his heavenly Father could do 'exceeding abundantly beyond all that we ask or think' (Eph 3:20).

We find Jesus standing on the shore of the lake, calling to the disciples, and asking what their catch had been during the night. On hearing their reply he asks them to cast their nets on the other side of the boat. One can just imagine their groans of complaint and cynical comments as they set about doing what Jesus had commanded them. Within a matter of moments, however, the excellence of the miracle began to startle them. Not only did Jesus give them a catch, but such a large haul that the nets began to break and the boat began to sink; there was such an abundance of blessing that another boat had to be brought alongside to cope with it.

Yet as we examine the blessing and excellence that Jesus through grace lavishes upon us, we can't help but notice the radical ruthless war he continually waged against shortcuts and compromise. Passing a fig tree and feeling hungry, he went across to it, and finding no fruit on it, he cursed it, causing it to wither and be the topic of much curious conversation among the disciples the next day. We see him in the temple, his anger rising, taking a whip in his hand and sending tables flying and animals and traders scampering as he expresses his displeasure at those who would desecrate his Father's house. You might say this all sounds very extreme; yes it is, and I am not advocating that we all become bull-in-the-china-shop Christians. What I am trying to say is that so often our compromise and mediocrity must surely sicken the Father as we shrink back from what he has shown us to do. You might also say that these moments of Jesus with the fig tree and the traders in the temple seem heartless, but in him there is measureless grace and love.

He stands and weeps outside Lazarus' tomb, his heart going out to the grieving friends and family. We see him standing in the extreme heat of dusty Jerusalem as the woman caught in the act of adultery is flung in front of him. After her accusers dropped their stones one by one and departed, Jesus gently asked her: 'Woman, where are they? Did no one condemn you?'

And she said, 'No one, Lord.'

And Jesus said, 'Neither do I condemn you, go your way. From now on, sin no more.'

Yet even with this example of an uncompromising, all-radical yet all-compassionate Saviour before us, we as Christians so often struggle to live in the realm of excellence. All too frequently you will meet someone who will tell you about a believer who promised to do something and broke his word. This seems to happen in the area of rendering a service, often in business, and you will hear, 'Oh, Christian businesses are unreliable.' This must truly grieve the heart of the Father, particularly when he gave us such a perfect example in Jesus. It saddens me too when sometimes at large Christian conferences, I meet someone who says, 'I just sneaked out from work for a few hours to attend this session,' not realising that they do their work as unto God and take their wages from him. They don't even realise that taking time off from work, without permission, even in the name of the Lord, is stealing from God and their employer.

God calls us to be reliable, even in those things which are unseen to other people and the general public. One of the areas that God challenged Carol and me about early on in our road ministry, was that we were faithfully to do the things that we told people we did. For example, we would have a regular daily schedule, and on the days designated for my being out on the road, I would ensure that I was out there on time and for a particular time span. Some days would be extremely hot, making walking a test of endurance; other days would be cold, or windy and people who accompanied me or met with me would often express surprise at my being out in those extreme conditions. My reply would simply be, 'The weather might have changed, but God hasn't changed his mind. He didn't tell me to walk if the sun was shining, or if it wasn't raining, or if it was a beautiful calm day without any wind; he simply said, "Go".' As Christians we need to be reliable in both word and deed and not compromise on that which we promise the Father and others we will do. Being out on the road far from familiar surroundings, we find ourselves continually tempted by the enemy's weapons of mediocrity and compromise. Constantly, therefore, we have to wage war in the Spirit realm against the principalities and powers that would try and get us to water down what God has called us to.

One of the areas where Jesus continually exhorted us was in our witness. He said,

> You are the light of the world. A city set on a hill cannot be hidden. Nor do men light a lamp, and put it under the peck measure, but on the lampstand; and it gives light to all who are in the house. Let your light shine before men in such a way that they may see your good works, and glorify your Father who is in heaven (Mt 5:14–16).

We are also reminded in the word that if we shrink back, the Lord's soul has no pleasure in us (Heb 10:38). Bearing in mind these commands, we attempt to spread his love abroad in whatever situation we find ourselves.

On one occasion we were in the little seaside village of Port Alfred, parked in a well-known caravan park particularly popular with holiday-makers from upcountry. The owner of the caravan park was a big burly bearded man, something of an intellectual, who had taken early retirement from his profession as a top advertising executive in Johannesburg. He would regularly do his rounds of the caravan park shirtless, displaying a well-cultivated tan and accompanied by his equally burly dog. The purpose of these rounds was to ensure that all was going smoothly in what was often a rather crowded caravan park, and, in addition, to perform a public relations function. However, I couldn't help feeling that he gave the area where our caravan was parked a wide berth. Apparently, he didn't want this globe-trotting footwasher to get his hands on him. His wife, however, was excited by all that we were involved in, and would keep him well-posted about our footwashing escapades. Each day we would continue to reach out and be friendly to him, but he would warily circle us, keeping his distance.

One day we received a request from his wife to come and pray through their house and over their children as their whole family had continually been dogged by one illness after another to the point where they could no longer endure it. Carol and I readily agreed to go to the house on condition that her husband was present. At the due time we arrived and were welcomed by the large burly man and his wife. As we sat down to chat, the man unleashed a barrage of intellectual New Age-type questions at me in a very calculated, controlled and intelligent way. We sat for the next two hours and reasoned back and forth, and I felt a little of what Paul must have felt when he went to the temple and debated the Scriptures day in, day out, with the Pharisees. He presented arguments like, 'There is a force of light and a force of darkness within the universe, but for anybody to call those forces a person or spirits would be presumptuous.' He argued that these forces create reproduction and nature and that all that takes place is accounted for by them. He queried what right Christians had to claim that Jesus was the only way to God. Quietly I reasoned, simply quoting the word in reply.

Finally after two-and-a-half hours, I pointed out to him that he had nothing to lose by praying and asking Jesus if he were real, to reveal himself to him. As we prayed, I could hardly contain my excitement, knowing that God is always faithful to his word. As he prayed, asking God to reveal himself to him, I couldn't help feeling that he had just placed the final nail in the coffin of all his intellectual arguments. With that, Carol, I, and his wife laid hands on and prayed over the children, after which we moved through each room in the house, binding in the name of Jesus any spirits assigned against their family. As we left their house that day, Carol and I felt we were standing on tiptoe waiting to see what the Holy Spirit would do.

Some months elapsed and we lost touch with this dear

couple, having moved several hundred kilometres further down the coast towards Cape Town. Then, unexpectedly and surprisingly, I received a message that the husband was lying desperately ill in a Port Elizabeth hospital and was asking to see me. During this crisis, as the Lord had very clearly got his attention, he had begun to reflect on our conversation. He had come to realise through the dramatic sequence of events that had taken place in and around his hospitalisation and severe illness, that he never could have come through without an active and living Saviour. During this time he dramatically surrendered his life to Jesus. A short time later, when I phoned him, it was amazing for me to hear the same voice that had previously uttered cynicisms against Jesus, now praising the Lord and telling me of the wonderful dealings of God in his life. Enthusiastically he went on to announce, 'Praise the Lord, brother, tonight we had a "Jericho march" around our caravan park and we could hear demons screaming. They fled parts of the park where the curse of death had been over a small dam where two little children once drowned.' Stunned, I held the telephone receiver away from my ear and looked at it. I couldn't believe what I was hearing. Jesus had radically turned this man inside out.

Some months later, Carol and I were privileged to be able to sit with him and his wife in their home and hear the stories of how the Lord had been able to change their lives and how he was assisting in the building of a church in a nearby poverty-stricken community. We could only thank the Lord that he had faithfully answered all that we asked in the Father's name, all because we had not shrunk back and compromised but had chosen to shine before men, even under adverse conditions.

Areas of testing and shrinking back often come in those things which are most tender to us and closest to our hearts. We often also get tested in the very things that we claim to stand for most. One of the areas that I have always been most emphatic about as we have been out on the road, is that if my family is not as God wants it to be I have nothing to say to anyone. I truly believe my family to be my first ministry and that God never calls half a flesh; he only calls a whole flesh. Thus he wouldn't call me without calling Carol, and in fact, he wouldn't call Carol and myself without calling our children. As we travelled throughout the land we always said that I alone was not called to this ministry but that God had called us as a family. Often, on reflection, this appeared to be one of our strongest areas of testimony in many of the churches where we ministered.

When as a family we started our pilgrimage, I naively believed we would be finished in about six months. As I have explained, the Lord had other ideas, and my pace was rather different from that which I had originally intended. When you have a family with two children in high school, you can make a plan for six months. When the plan goes beyond six months, you can stretch it to nine months, and even at the very extreme, to a year. But when it gets to eighteen months, the rules of the game change completely, and one rapidly discovers that a totally new strategy is required.

We noticed that although we were often in different churches every week and our children were making many lovely friends, a tangible loneliness and longing began to arise within them. For example, they desired regular friendships that could be maintained day by day; they wanted a set school with friends they could interact with and a youth group they could participate in. They wanted to know that they had their own church to go to each Sunday and a regular daily routine that could be maintained. Not least, Carol and I were growing more and more concerned about the quality of the education which we were able to give the children while out on the road.

It seemed strange that it was not so much ourselves as the children who were feeling the effects of all these irregularities. As the months wore on, the pressure of this particular problem seemed to weigh more and more heavily upon us as a family. We prayed and talked many hours about it, not knowing what to do. Eventually we realised that if one of the children were to go back home, they would both have to go, as we had noticed that during one short absence of our daughter, our son had become extremely lonely.

What were we to do? We knew for sure that God had called us to this rather unusual but deeply fulfilling ministry. Many times we had seen his hand upon us and his reassurance as towns and cities had been moved by what he had called us to do. Were we now supposed to pack up halfway and abort all that we believed God had called us to? The question I was asking myself was, 'How can I possibly continue to claim that my family is my first ministry if they aren't even with me?' I would look like a hypocrite if I claimed one thing and yet lived another. I wrestled to understand what was happening.

Finally, the decision was reached. The children would return home to Johannesburg and live with Carol's parents, Doug and Joan Faragher. Dad Faragher had always run a Hebrew-model home with an extended family, and our children had always felt that it was their other home. Carol's one younger sister, Colleen, was only seven years older than our daughter Carynne, and Dad Faragher had always treated our children like his own. It was searingly painful as I stood and watched my children drive back to Johannesburg, and that night I just lay in the bunk of my caravan and wept. Night after night, I would lie in that bunk and cry, not understanding what God was doing, and what was happening to me. During that time our dear friend, Laura Charlewood, I think sensing the pain I was feeling, handed me this beautiful story by Watchman Nee which deeply ministered healing to my spirit.

My flesh and my heart faileth: but God is the strength of my heart and my portion for ever (Ps 73:26, KJV).

A brother I know was called to go on a preaching tour of some months. His wife, to whom he was very attached, was in poor health at the time. A friend had sent me with a last-minute letter to him, and as I came in sight of his house, unseen by him, I observed him come out, walk a little distance, then stop, and after a little hesitation begin slowly to return. I did not wait, but sensing his conflict of spirit I went ahead to the river-boat by another route. On his arrival there I handed him the letter with the words, 'May the Lord bless you,' and his answer revealed that he was quite at peace. When after some months he came back from the tour I alluded to the incident. 'Yes,' he confessed, 'as I stood there, I felt I could not leave her and the children with no help and very little money, but as I was retracing my steps the verse came to me: "No man, having put his hand to the plough, and looking back, is fit for the kingdom of God." So I turned again and went down to the boat.' To hold on to the plough while wiping our tears—that is Christianity. (Watchman Nee, *A Table in the Wilderness* Kingsway: Eastbourne, 1965)

The children, I think, felt a little more secure about the move than did Carol and I, as they looked forward to the prospect of staying with Granny and Pa, as the Faraghers were affectionately known. Carol's mum was a typical mother hen who had a wonderful servant heart and would do anything to ensure the comfort of her grandchildren. It seemed to be an ideal set-up for the children, in that Carol's parents didn't live far from our church, which also housed the children's school. It was near their friends and central to the youth group to which they belonged. One of the deals that we had struck with the children in our many hours of discussion was that during their school holidays they would fly down to us no matter where we were. The agreement was that in the first week after their return, I would not spend any time out on the road, I would not take on any preaching engagements and we would discourage any visitors to the caravan. In other words, it would be their week. We agreed they could choose the agenda, and we would do whatever they wanted to do.

In this way we believed that God would redeem the time for us as a family. I might add that God did indeed redeem that time and during the ensuing holidays we had some of the best times we have ever enjoyed as a family. The children certainly organised action-packed weeks including items such as paddle-skiing, cave explorations and watching world cup soccer on television. The other thing that thrilled us was to discover as time passed that both children were becoming far more academically competent, and that their school marks were improving dramatically. All this however did not diminish the fact that Carol and I still struggled with not having the children with us.

Our course, to a lesser or greater extent, now seemed to be reset and it appeared that we had endured the test, not giving in to the missiles of compromise that were raining down on us. Little did we realise, however, that an even bigger blow was yet to come. It started at the end of June 1990. Carol and I had driven up the coast from Mossel Bay where the caravan was parked, to catch a late-night flight to Durban, where I was due to hold a series of outreach meetings with a number of churches for the weekend. At Port Elizabeth airport we decided that we would phone the children in Johannesburg to find out if all was well. While chatting to Carynne on the phone, Carol sensed an urgent note in her voice as she said, 'Mummy, Granny is very ill. I know she won't tell you because she doesn't want to alarm you, but please, Mummy, you must come.'

Carol instantly knew that Carynne wouldn't be an alarmist and that neither Carol's mum nor her dad would in any way want to place us under any pressure or concern. Carol's mum was only sixty-two at the time and was the youngest of all our parents by a long stretch. She had not been very well lately, but we had not felt up to that point that there was any cause for alarm. However, the urgency in Carynne's voice allowed the Holy Spirit to jerk us to attention. Both of us felt immediately that Carol should go, but what were we to do? We had the tickets booked and our plane was due to leave in twenty-five minutes for Durban. We decided that Carol would fly to Durban, sleep the night there and that early the next morning we would try to get her on a flight to Johannesburg. The following day, by God's grace, we easily managed to get Carol onto a flight to Johannesburg, while I stayed on in Durban to continue with the hectic weekend's schedule.

On the Monday, I phoned Johannesburg, to have Carol inform me that her mother was to be hospitalised. She felt however that I should take the late night flight back to Port Elizabeth, saying that she would join me as soon as possible. Thus on Monday night I found myself sleeping in Port Elizabeth. On Tuesday night I slept in the town of George, some 350 kilometres away. The following morning I was due to address a gathering of some forty pastors and ministers from the town of George, and immediately after the meeting I phoned Carol, who said that her mother was due to go in for investigative surgery. She asked if I would come up to Johannesburg, over 1,000 kilometres away, without delay.

Fortunately, one of the pastors from George was due to travel by car to Johannesburg immediately and before I knew what had happened, I was driving up to Johannesburg. It all happened so fast, I wasn't quite sure where I was or what was taking place! The last five or six nights had been midnight stints for me. Each night in a different bed, often in a different town, and now totally unexpectedly, I was heading back to Johannesburg, with my caravan parked in one town, my car in another, and myself with only a weekend's supply of clothing headed in the opposite direction! Once again it was midnight as we arrived in Johannesburg. The following day, Mum went in for surgery and we waited on tenter-hooks for the surgeon's results. Finally the surgeon broke the news to my dear wife and her family that Mum had terminal cancer and that there was nothing they could do to help her. They said it was too advanced for them even to suggest any form of chemotherapy and that she had between three months and a year to live.

Dave and Carol

The family was stunned. Reeling from the shock, we tried to rise up in faith. We were asking every kind of question. 'Why, Lord, when she is so young? What could it be? Why should this happen?' So the questions flowed, with seemingly very few answers. I decided to stay a day or two until we had broken to Mum the news of the outcome of the exploratory operation. One day while visiting her in hospital, the Lord gave Carol a beautiful opportunity to speak openly about our security in the Lord, to talk with Mum about eternity and to carefully check out her assurance of salvation. All these things seemed to be in place and Mum with complete calm was able to ask Carol questions about the cancer within her body.

At that, I knew it was time to return to the road. Carol said that she would just allow her mum to return home and be settled before joining me once again on the road within a few days. However, this was not to be. On my return to the road ministry, life seemed rather unsettled and uncertain. I did not know how Mum's health would hold up and after several days, I began to miss Carol desperately. I realised just how much a part of our ministry Carol was and the vital role that she played in backing me up, fetching and carrying me, upholding me in prayer and speaking God's word of life to me continually.

Daily I continued to bombard heaven for Mum's healing. My mind raced back across all the people whom we had prayed for; miracle after miracle that we had seen by God's grace flashed through my mind. I could see the faces of those cancer sufferers we had prayed for, and whom God had set free, but now it was our own mother and somehow there was a dynamic at work that I had not grasped.

One day while battling in prayer, I came across a verse which set me free:

For this perishable must put on the imperishable and this mortal must put on immortality. But when this perishable will have put on the imperishable, and this mortal will have put on immortality, then will come about the saying that is written, 'DEATH IS SWALLOWED UP IN VICTORY. O DEATH, WHERE IS YOUR VICTORY? O DEATH, WHERE IS YOUR STING?' (1 Cor 15:53–55).

Here, I suddenly realised, was the key. As mortals, when we receive Christ as our Lord and Saviour—at that point of being born again—death is swallowed up in victory and loses its sting. But yet there was one question still pounding through my mind. I knew that the word declared that God wanted Mum to be in good health, just as her soul prospered (3 Jn 1:2). The battle remained. How were we to pray? Suddenly the Holy Spirit began to show me that while Mum had breath in her body, God wanted her to prosper and be in good health. Coming back to 1 Corinthians 15, however, he showed me that as Mum allowed her mortal to put on immortality, she was living from that moment in eternity and it made no difference to God whether she lived in her earthsuit or whether she lived in the spirit realm in the heavenlies with him. I could feel relief flooding me. We could continue to pray for divine health for Mum and trust that as she knew the Lord, it made no difference to him whether she lived or died. Yet he showed me once again, that for the millions who did not know him, it made all the difference if they were not saved. We needed to grasp this firmly as a family. If we did not understand this, then we had never truly understood what Jesus did when he died for us on the cross.

Things were to move far faster now than any of us expected. Ten days after my return to the road, while in the beautiful little Southern Cape town of Riversdale, one of the local pastors came to the caravan with an urgent message for me to phone Carol. I rushed to the nearest telephone and Carol, with a quivering voice, said that I needed to come quickly as the doctor didn't think that Mum would make it through the night. I had nearly a three hour chase to the nearest airport to get on a flight at one o'clock in the morning, and arrived back in

Johannesburg just after 3 am. As I walked into the room, the whole family was gathered, with all Carol's brothers and sisters and their respective partners. As I set eyes on Mum I was absolutely staggered by the amount that she had deteriorated in just fifteen days. Nevertheless, she was to hang on for the next five days as we kept vigil at her bedside, simply praying and speaking the word over her continually day and night, until just three weeks after the diagnosis, she closed her eyes and stepped into the arms of the Father.

Once Mum's funeral service had taken place, and the time was right for me to return to the road, the next major test was to confront us. Carol felt strongly that her father needed her around the house during this difficult period and that she would therefore be unable to rejoin me on the road. In addition, we realised that we simply couldn't leave Dad alone to care for our children. Carol would have to remain there. It was a bitter blow, the second in a row to our family unity. Not only was I not to have my children with me, but now I was to be separated from my wife too.

As I lay in my caravan bunk that first night after bidding Carol goodbye, I couldn't help feeling that our testimony was being eroded. What kind of a minister was I being to my family now, when we had set out in such glorious oneness only to be reduced to a situation where they were all back in Johannesburg and I was all alone out on the road? It seemed so lonely. What was I to do? Was I to compromise and pack up just four months from the finish? Daily I could hear the words of Jesus ringing through my soul, 'Anyone after putting his hand to the plough and turning back is not fit for the kingdom of God.' Day by day I struggled on, not realising that God was about to make a way for me as he confirmed once again in my heart that as a family we were not called to mediocrity.

12

Possessing the Land

The wind rippled through the wheat fields surrounding me as far as the eye could see as I walked steadily westwards through the Southern Cape. Mossel Bay was behind me now, the last large town that I would cross before reaching Cape Town. Carol and I had always reflectively said that once Mossel Bay was past, we were on the home straight, even though some 400 kilometres still remained, interspersed with several small towns and many hills. The gentle rustle of the wind through the wheat was punctuated by the staccato crunch-crunch of my shoes on the gravel, as I maintained a steady pace. I was truly enjoying the sense of being out in the open with God's beauty all about me and was praying quietly in the Spirit, when out of the corner of my eye, I became aware of something moving alongside me. A large ostrich with its rather awkward trotting action and bobbing head was keeping pace with me. Blessed by having this unexpected companion, I stopped and turned to it.

'Having a good day out here?' I enquired.

Perfectly on cue, the ostrich came closer and began to perform a dance that would not have been out of place at a performance of *Swan Lake* at the Vienna Opera House. Bobbing and weaving rhythmically, it pirouetted back and forth, ducking its head beneath its feathers, then gracefully extending it. Feeling highly flattered to be the sole spectator of this wonderful command performance, I watched for some minutes then, praising

God for his magnificent creation, I picked up the cross and bowl and went on my way. The day continued to be one of those triumphant ones in the Lord and later that afternoon I was collected at the roadside by a pastor from a neighbouring town.

Elated by my earlier experience, I began enthusiastically to relate how this female ostrich had blessed me by performing such a magnificent dance, when suddenly the pastor interrupted me.

'Umm, Dave, I think you've got a problem!' he said with a grin. I looked at him rather puzzled. 'Firstly,' he said, 'that wasn't a female ostrich; from your description it was a male, and secondly, that was a mating dance he was performing for you. I think you've got a problem because that ostrich obviously has a crush on you.' Needless to say, the car rocked with laughter as we travelled back towards the spot where my caravan was parked.

Now with Cape Town almost within grasp, as it were, I started to examine a strange dynamic taking place in my emotions. Initially, when we had set out on the road we thought that I could walk seven days a week, sixteen hours a day and that we would reach Cape Town in six months. However, God rapidly proved to me that our ways are not his ways and that there was much life to touch within each town. There were projects, plans and ministry that he had initiated almost every step of the way, plus major outreaches in many of the cities I was to pass through. In addition, there had been the trauma of the death of Carol's mum, and the consequent change of plans that this unforeseen event had precipitated. But praise God, he made a way when there seemed to be no way. In Carol's absence, friends and local churches rallied round, providing invaluable back-up. Gary, my pastor friend from Durban, came down twice to assist, and my precious mum and dad stayed with me for a month as I neared Cape Town. It was lovely to have my parents with me from a spiritual support point of view. Some of the earliest recollections I have of my childhood are of my mother faithfully turning aside each day to spend time reading the Bible in the presence of the Father, drawing from the well of his sustaining life-giving love even when things were tough.

After some eighteen months on the road, we had begun to realise that this wasn't merely some short-term mission but, in fact, a call to a whole new way of life. We were keenly aware that God had changed us as a family and given us a deep love for the people on the streets and for the broader body of Christ. In my mind, therefore, Cape Town had become a far-off place that I would reach some day, I guess a bit like death. We know that one day we will die and go to heaven, but for now we live on this earth and it's other people who die; that sort of thing simply doesn't happen to us. Now suddenly, abruptly, Cape Town was just up ahead. To me it felt almost as if it were in the twinkling of an eye and I guess that in many ways, in my spirit, I wished that the road just continued on from this tip of Africa towards the South Pole.

As I started to think about Cape Town through the several hundred kilometres that I still had to walk, I realised that in most cities where God had laid something on my heart for that city, it had more often than not taken place once I had actually reached it. As I asked God, 'Lord, is there anything for this city?' he would sometimes reveal to me that there was a plan, and sometimes not. If there was nothing, we would simply walk through the streets of the city, ministering to those whom the Lord gave us the privilege of touching, and then moving on, for I do not want to be in anything that God isn't in. I never want to crank something up just because it's man's good idea.

I began to realise, however, that in this instance we would need to know well in advance what God was planning for Cape Town. Many people were writing, phoning and contacting us from around the country, asking what would be happening when I reached Cape Town as they would like to be there. My immediate response to the Lord was, 'Lord, if there is nothing, I am happy just to walk quietly into Cape Town and head on home, but somehow I do not believe that you would bring me this far and not end with that which would be glorifying to yourself.' So in the ensuing weeks, I set about praying fervently into the matter and waiting on the Lord to find out what he had on his heart for Cape Town. Finally after much battling in the Spirit, the picture began to take shape as once again, ever-faithfully, God pointed me to his word. I sensed the Lord directing me to three particular places.

The first was where Moses and Aaron had sent a man from each of the twelve tribes of Israel to go and spy out the Promised Land.

When they returned from spying out the land, at the end of forty days, they proceeded to come to Moses and Aaron and to all the congregation of the sons of Israel in the wilderness of Paran, at Kadesh; and they brought back word to them and to all the congregation and showed them the fruit of the land. Thus they told him, and said, 'We went in to the land where you sent us; and it certainly does flow with milk and honey, and this is its fruit. Nevertheless, the people who live in the land are strong, and the cities are fortified and very large; and moreover, we saw the descendants of Anak there. Amalek is living in the land of the Negev and the Hittites and the Jebusites and the Amorites are living in the hill country, and the Canaanites are living by the sea and by the side of the Jordan.' Then Caleb quieted the people before Moses, and said, 'We should by all means go up and take possession of it, for we shall surely overcome it.' But the men who had gone up with him said, 'We are not able to go up against the people for they are too strong for us.' So they gave out to the sons of Israel a bad report of the land which they had spied out, saying 'The land through which we have gone, in spying it out, is a land that devours its inhabitants; and all the people whom we saw in it are men of great size. There also we saw the Nephilim [the sons of Anak are part of the Nephilim]; and we became like grasshoppers in our own sight, and so we were in their sight' (Num 13:25–33).

I love the way that Caleb chose to keep his eye on God and refused to focus on the problem. The story then goes on to show how the people of Israel rebelled against Moses and Aaron and finally God's judgement came upon them. God prohibited them from entering the Promised Land, saying that these people

> shall by no means see the land which I swore to their fathers, nor shall any of those who spurned Me see it. But my servant Caleb, because he has had a different spirit and followed Me fully, I will bring into the land which he entered and his descendants shall take possession of it.

As I reflected on Cape Town I began to realise that much of this situation applied. One of the most picturesque cities in the world, it had nevertheless been dogged by false gods, such as the New Age movement, the spirit of homosexuality, Islam and much more. It was a place where so often the prevailing spirit was one where people chose to worship the creation of God rather than the God of creation. Often the Christians there had either been neutralised or had shrunk back because of the size of the enemy. As I pondered the Mother City nestled beneath the legendary Table Mountain, with sprawling vineyards across the peninsula, and all the magnificence of the heritage of the beautiful Cape architecture and character, I had to concede that indeed it was a land flowing with milk and honey. I then focused again on God's dealings with the people of Israel and how God had said Caleb was a man of a different spirit. I began to sense that God was calling out the Christians of Cape Town with a different spirit. Caleb's words declaring 'we shall by all means go up and take possession of it' rang in my mind.

Cape Town had recently been the scene of a major confrontation between Christians and New Agers when the latter had rigged up their totem poles on top of Table Mountain and a group of 'budding Elijah' Christians had promptly gone up and knocked the totem poles down, breaking them up. The situation was fanned by the fact that the mayor himself was a New Ager and had insisted that the case be taken to court. Emotions were running fairly high in the city, to say the least. Another thing that really bothered me, notwithstanding the splendour of the architecture of the Rhodes Memorial which stands proudly overlooking Cape Town, was the inscription beneath the statue of Rhodes, reading, 'His spirit broods over this place.' The statue was erected in honour of Cecil John Rhodes, an extremely wealthy pioneer and mining magnate during the 1800s as well as the founder of Rhodesia, now known as Zimbabwe. Rhodes' spirit was indeed also one of those that prevailed strongly over Cape Town, where people are caught up in a yuppie-type materialism that attempts to create a mystique of its own. It was widely rumoured that Cecil Rhodes had been a homosexual, and this spirit too runs rampant within the city, to the abhorrence of God.

Once again my mind drifted back to the magnificence of Table Mountain with her famed table-cloth of cloud. With three things in my mind as I prayed, the picture of the table-cloth on the mountain, Caleb's words, 'We shall by all means go up and take possession of it,' and a sense that God was calling out a people of a different spirit, I suddenly pictured a blanket of prayer covering the down-town area of Cape Town. That was it; that's what it was to be! God would throw a blanket of prayer across the down-town city of Cape Town as a testimony, as the Christians took possession of the land. I had a picture of Christians praying on every street corner in down-town Cape Town. What a glorious testimony it would be. But how would this be done?

The second place that the Lord then showed me in his word was where he was instructing the disciples and said, 'Give to everyone who asks of you' (Lk 6:30). This verse had constantly bothered me for the past two years and more that I had trodden the subcontinent. Every day I had people asking me for something or other; every day I asked the Lord, 'How do you give to everyone who asks?' The thing that troubled me was that Jesus didn't say, 'Give to some,' or 'Give when you can,' but 'Give to everyone.' As I pondered this yet again, the Lord went on to create the most beautiful picture in my heart. I saw in the Spirit the Christians of Cape Town at a central point down-town, taking care of every need that came their way, offering salvation to all who asked, clothes to all who asked, love to all who asked, security to all who asked, restoration of marriage to all who asked—and all this in the name of Jesus to the glory of the Father. But once again the question was, 'How?'

The third dimension of what God was pointing me to in his word came as I prayed, reflecting with a heart overflowing with deep gratitude for all that the Lord had done, as he and I had trodden the subcontinent together. I realised how he had put the powers of darkness under his feet as the words from Luke's Gospel rang through my spirit: 'And as He said this, all His opponents were being humiliated; and *the entire multitude was rejoicing over all the glorious things being done by Him*' (Lk 13:17, italics mine).

I realised that indeed Satan had been humiliated as Jesus had so often won the victory, and even here as we faced this final frontier of the powers of darkness, the multitudes would once again rejoice over the glorious things that Jesus had done. I had a growing conviction that we needed to end with a time of high praise to bring glory to Jesus. Once again the question was, 'How?' How was I to co-ordinate these three major events in the same week: Christians praying on every down-town street corner, assembling together to meet every need and, finally, an event of glorious praise to God? How was I, living out of a caravan at the roadside, to do it without a slick administrative structure? How was I to do it without a telephone or fax back-up? But God in his faithfulness and wisdom had spoken it and surely he would see that it would come to pass.

Slowly, over the weeks to come, God proved faithful to his word. As I darted through at weekends to preach at various churches, at breakfasts and other functions, people would come under conviction as they realised what God was saying. Gradually the numbers steadily increased as churches in the broader body of Christ across the Peninsula rallied and spoke out their commitment. Finally the stage was set. There was nothing more that I could do except simply trust the Spirit of the Lord to bring to pass what he had spoken into being.

Whenever I begin to take myself too seriously, the Lord brings me back to earth with a bump and makes me laugh at myself. While involved in these hectic long-range preparations for all that God was revealing for Cape Town, I continued my journey along the roadside. Finally the day came when I was about to stand at the top of the magnificent Sir Lowry's Pass and catch my first roadside glimpse of the Cape Peninsula way below, stretching through to the Table Mountain. My pastor friend Gary, from Durban, was once again accompanying me, along with a young couple called Barry and Trish. Trish had been in many ways like a daughter to Carol and myself as she had lived in our home for some time before marrying Barry and moving to Cape Town.

I decided it would be a grand spiritual moment for all of us to meet together on top of Sir Lowry's Pass and celebrate communion as a truly fitting act of thanksgiving to God.

The last leg of the climb to the top of Sir Lowry's was incredibly steep and I was drenched in perspiration. It was a lovely sight finally to see Gary walking down to meet me, as that meant the summit was near. As we crested the last rise together, we discovered that we were a few minutes earlier than arranged, and Barry and Trish had not yet arrived. To pass the time, we decided Gary would take some pictures of me with the cross and bowl. He took the camera out of the car and, leaving the door open, moved around to begin taking photographs.

Suddenly, to my consternation, I saw a huge baboon bound across behind Gary, jump into the car and exit with the bread and grape juice which we had brought along for our solemn occasion. Backing off a few paces, he sat down with legs astride and commenced piously to break the bread, keeping the grape juice near at hand. We both attempted to retrieve our property, but the baboon displayed an awesome set of canine teeth and came at us. Very rapidly and submissively we beat a headlong retreat in total deference to the one now fully in control of the communion elements. Eventually we began to do the only thing possible in the situation— see the funny side of it. We laughed and laughed until our sides ached, while Gary used his camera to record the solemn occasion for posterity. I couldn't help thinking that if there were any onlookers, they wouldn't have any difficulty discerning who looked spiritual and who were the monkeys.

It didn't need any long deliberation for us to decide to abandon our event as more large baboons emerged from their rocky lairs to join the party. Gary leaped into the car and drove off, while I hastily resumed my walk— straight into a swarm of wild bees. What with keeping a wary eye open for baboons, trying to avoid getting stung to death or run over by high-speed passing traffic, it was all very undignified. I guess Jesus and his disciples too must have had occasions like this, when all they could do was laugh.

Time passed quickly after that, and at last the day dawned when we were to head off into down-town Cape Town for the start of what God had previously revealed. As I dressed, the first light of dawn creeping through the caravan window, I started to reflect on what had taken place over the preceding couple of weeks.

After the encounter with the baboons on Sir Lowry's Pass, I had made my way across the Peninsula via Somerset West, cutting across into the large coloured area of Mitchell's Plain and then up into the utter squalor of the notorious Crossroads Squatter Camp. My times in Crossroads had been rather bumpy as the inhabitants were rioting and many of the tin shanties had been razed to the ground, gutted by fire, as I walked through this tragic area. I then crossed into Constantia with all its magnificence and grandeur, and found it hard to believe that these two places could be on the same planet, let alone so close together. From Constantia I had walked down into the picturesque village of Hout Bay, enjoying the serene beauty of this little fishing harbour, before winding my way further around the magnificent coastline. Then it was up over the neck of Table Mountain and down into the city.

All these memories and others avalanched through my mind as I dressed in the semi-darkness, preparing myself for the week-long finale of my walk through Southern Africa. I recalled how, as I had come across that neck of Table Mountain and seen the city spread out at my feet, I had just wept. All the pent-up emotion accumulated in over two years on the road seemed to burst out as the end literally came into view. I remembered the thrill as I moved into down-town Cape Town and the first person I met as I turned into the street leading to the Houses of Parliament was my dear friend Graham Lambert, whose feet I had washed more than two years before outside the Union Buildings in Pretoria. Then at Cape Town's Houses of Parliament themselves, there was the delight of rejoicing in the manifest presence of my heavenly Father as I was simultaneously honoured by the presence of my earthly father. My dad, who had planted the seeds of the rich heritage of the mighty God and his precious Son within my heart, was there to share the moment with me.

Now it was all systems go for the prayer blanket to be thrown over Cape Town, as well as the Jesus Junction—as we subsequently named it—and the culminating Explosion of Praise. To make my joy complete, my precious wife Carol was able to join me for this last part of the pilgrimage, followed a few days later by my children.

At about 5.50 am, early-morning quiet still reigned in Cape Town's streets as Christians began to converge on Greenmarket Square, signifying the start of the time of prayer. By just after 6 am the group had assembled and we triumphantly held up five loaves of bread and two raw fish as we made a prophetic statement that the Spirit which prevailed within us would multiply, as well as the numbers that would come in the following days of that week. After preaching and joyously singing to the glory of God, much to the bewilderment of passers-by, we sent the believers out onto each street corner in twos, with a list of guidelines concerning things that they should pray into for the city.

This marked the start of a glorious event as we met for the next four days in the early morning at Greenmarket Square before the people dispersed onto the corners of the city. What a beautiful peace there was each morning as the Christians prayed and the passers-by on their way to work saw the glorious witness of the peace of the Lord about the streets as we were throwing a blanket of prayer across the down-town city of Cape Town.

During that time we saw people come to salvation on their way to work; others would stop and join in on the street corners as they were moving to their places of employment. Some mornings it was difficult even to get the Christians to stop praying and despatch them to their different tasks in time for work and to avoid falling foul of their employers. One thing that God was reminding us in those days was that in obedience we truly were going in and taking possession of the land, faithfully living in obedience to the words of Jesus where he said, 'You shall be My witnesses.'

As the week progressed, the days proved to be exceptionally pressurised. I would rise at 4.45 each morning and proceed to the blanket of prayer, after which I would spend the day with a television crew from the national network, going through squatter camps, the docks and mountain passes, before rushing back down-town once more to where the Jesus Junction was taking place. One of the things I never do with the media is contrive anything as far as I can possibly help it. I would rather that they tag along and that we trust the Holy Spirit to do his work, ensuring a genuine record of what

God is doing. This, however, didn't make my life any easier as I was very aware that the hire of cameramen, crew and equipment is a costly exercise and that catch-as-catch-can filming is very time-consuming.

The purpose of the Jesus Junction, as described earlier, was to meet needs. The results which were evident each night from early evening until late were far more amazing than we could ever have contemplated. Each evening we had two churches from different denominations as the anchor on the square as we ministered to every form of human need and degradation that one could ever imagine. The response from the churches was overwhelming and the support was wonderful as we saw several hundred Christians minister to the down-and-outs, the homeless, the hungry and the street-children. We saw many come to salvation and delivered from their bondages. The Christians literally touched life in the raw, as we plundered hell. One beautiful moment was when we saw one of the street-children who had been on the run for over three years reconciled to her parents. Another was when we had the privilege of taking a man who had been down and out, putting him up in a hotel for the night, providing him with clothes and a haircut and taking him into one of the Christian families' homes as we helped him seek employment.

One evening as I arrived at the square, I was introduced to a lady and her sister, the mother of an eleven-year-old boy, who had been paralysed all his life. The lady had read a large newspaper article that the *Argus* newspaper had carried on what was taking place, and they had brought the child for healing. As I observed the child in his paralysed state, I must confess that my faith at that point didn't exceed the size of a mustard seed. After a while as a large crowd gathered, I placed the cross and bowl in the centre of the cobbled square and Carol held the child on her lap as we knelt around the bowl and began to storm heaven for his healing. Somehow it seemed that the more we prayed the larger the crowd seemed to get, and the weaker my faith became. As, however, I simply begged and pleaded with God, gathering up the crumbs under his table, the Holy Spirit seemed to break through, and finally as the crowd pressed in on every side, I sensed the quiet voice of the Spirit saying to me, 'If you believe he is healed, then stand him up.' I held the little boy around the waist and stood him up in the bowl, saying, 'In the name of Jesus, be healed.' I let him go and, to my horror, his rubbery legs collapsed beneath him. I couldn't help but feel that this was Satan lying to me, so once again I lifted him up by his waist and said, 'In the name of Jesus, stand.' My faith was rapidly diminishing as for the second time I saw his little legs buckle beneath him. A third time I spoke to him, saying, 'In the name of Jesus, stand.'

Suddenly I felt him push himself upright as the energising power of the Holy Spirit surged through his paralysed limbs. He stood up unaided, taking a stumbling little step. I realised that, never having walked in his life, he would have to learn how. The crowd erupted into joyous cheering and clapping. Many wept, danced and jumped around as we rejoiced that before our very eyes, we had once more witnessed the miracle-working power of the living God.

Near the end of our nights down on the square with the Jesus Junction, I was wearily propping myself up against a tree, just enjoying all that was taking place in the presence of the Lord. It had been a demanding week and the physical exertion of it was starting to take its toll. Talk about burning one's candle at both ends—I felt like mine had been burning in the middle too. As I stood contentedly with the Lord, someone drew alongside me. It was one of the local ministers whom I had come to love and respect deeply.

'What are you feeling, Dave?' he asked.

My eyes started to rove around the square as my spirit began to categorise and reflect on what was going on all around me. A large group of about 150 Christians was standing on the square, some playing guitars, while people from every race were just worshipping with delight and joy as they reflected on Jesus. Across the square, two Kombis (minibuses) were standing. From one, free food was being issued to a queue of more than a hundred hungry people; the other had an equally long queue of people being sized up and given clothing.

My mind raced back to the very beginning of all of this: the call God had originally placed on my life when he had taken me to Luke's Gospel, chapter 4, where Jesus said, 'The Spirit of the Lord is upon me, he anointed me to preach the gospel to the poor.' There across the square I could see it being fulfilled. As I shifted my gaze, I saw Christians praying over people for deliverance from bondages and I realised that we were proclaiming *release to the captives*. Right over on the far side, another group was praying for the sick and we saw them being healed. I reflected on so much that had happened as people had come and reported miracles such as deaf ears being unstopped and I realised, yes, we were bringing healing and proclaiming *recovery of sight to the blind*. I saw the hobos and the street-children being ministered to and cared for and realised that we were *setting free those who were down-trodden*. Across the other side of the square I saw people coming to faith in Christ. I pondered on the many who had come to know Jesus with their feet in the bowl that week, and I realised that we were indeed *proclaiming the favourable year of the Lord*. Residents in the neighbouring hotels, tourists and top business executives had come down and found Jesus during those nights.

I turned to my minister friend whose question had prompted this reverie, and with a deep sense of gratitude I reflected with him that finally the Spirit of the Lord was starting to move in this area of my life. His word was true; it was beginning to be fulfilled in me.

With the Jesus Junction now concluded late on the Saturday night, we looked towards Sunday afternoon. This was the moment when I would finally carry the bowl for the last symbolic kilometre of my journey across Southern Africa into the Explosion of Praise which would glorify Jesus. Friends and family had gathered from all over South Africa. People had come from different parts of the Cape Province. Many of the churches in the Cape Town area had agreed to close their Sunday night services in order to join in this glorious event which we trusted would exalt the name of Jesus.

The idea had been originated when I had gone one day to meet with the President of Psalmody International, Tom Inglis, to ask if he would mind coming down from Johannesburg to co-ordinate a time of high praise to honour Jesus at the end of this pilgrimage. As soon as Tom and I got together, the Holy Spirit caused us to fire one another with enthusiasm. Rapidly, as we exchanged thoughts and ideas, the concept of an Explosion of Praise emerged whereby Tom would co-ordinate a different worship team coming on each half-hour, as people from all over would glorify Jesus.

The next idea was that two other well-known worship leaders would also participate in the Explosion of Praise. One was Dave Ornellas, who had formerly been a well-known South African entertainer. After coming to the Lord, he had become the pastor in charge of worship at the well-known large Rhema Bible Church in Johannesburg. Then he had become the pastor of a large church in Cape Town. The other worship leader would be the well-known 'Friends First' personality, Malcolm du Plessis. Both he and Dave Ornellas, it was subsequently agreed, would do a half-hour concert as part of the Explosion of Praise.

Finally, Sunday afternoon, three o'clock, arrived as my family and I drew up at the large Lighthouse Church in Parow. It had formerly been an entertainment theatre, and seated over 2,000 people. The pastor, Walty Snyman, had agreed to rig up a monitor in their 500-seater overflow hall just in case it was needed. The sight that greeted me as I arrived caused me to gasp in disbelief. I had thought that possibly we might start off with a couple of hundred people, who would come and go throughout the afternoon, as their own particular worship teams were leading, and that hopefully the

auditorium would begin to fill up towards the latter part
of the Explosion of Praise. Never in my wildest dreams
had I imagined the scene now before my eyes. Well
over half an hour before the event was due to start, the
place was jam-packed to capacity and before we even
began, the overflow was full too. I couldn't help feeling
embarrassed about the hundreds being turned away.
Then, as Tom introduced the first worship team, the
place erupted into worship. In all my life I have never
been in such worship. People jammed the aisles. The
front of the stage was packed with people worshipping
perpetually at fever pitch. After an hour and a half I
thought, 'This cannot go on; the people are going to
burst or drop,' when suddenly Malcolm du Plessis
appeared for his half-hour slot.

I was sure that Malcolm, who is renowned for his
praise parties, would continue the praise at fever pitch,
but he came with the most gentle, lilting piano playing
in the Spirit that I have ever experienced. His sensitivity
to the Spirit was so sweet that he brought a beautiful
peace and calm into the entire auditorium as people just
lingered restfully under the anointing of God's Spirit.
Then, praise erupted once more, continuing unabated
and building all the time throughout Tom Inglis' half-
hour slot. Finally Dave Ornellas got up and literally
grabbed the devil by the throat as he sang the famous
song, 'Radically Saved'. During Dave's time of ministering
with his family, which touched the hearts of many, I
slipped away with my family and the cross and bowl for
the symbolic last stage of my walk. At the end of Dave's
time of ministering in song, people poured out onto the
streets and literally thousands lined the pavement as we
walked the last kilometre of our long journey across
Southern Africa.

The more I walked and carried the cross, the more
excited the crowd became. They were grabbing me,
shaking my hand, hugging me, pushing me, gathering
around, praising, worshipping and dancing in the street.
The traffic ground to a halt in the overwhelming

enthusiasm that surrounded the cross and bowl as the crowd pushed and shoved, jostled and glorified God. I even became separated from Carol and my two teenagers, Carrie and Ronnie-Russ. The television camera crew who were trying to walk backwards filming me at a rather rapid pace, were also just about managing to keep on their feet. I never did see Carol and the children again until they finally reappeared, being swept along by the crowds through one of the side entrances of the auditorium. Praise the Lord, this was indeed a glorious moment. Even if we had wanted to stage a thing like this, we could never have organised what the Holy Spirit organised that night.

When the auditorium was once again jam-packed, I fell on my knees beside the cross and bowl and quietly gave thanks to the Lord for what he had done, before going on to reflect what God had accomplished as I had crossed the sub-continent. I did not want to preach for long because I wanted Jesus to get the glory; then once again, as Tom led a composite worship team with brass instruments, the crowd erupted into high worship and continued to glorify God. At the end they had been going for almost four and a half hours and still did not want to stop. It was a glimpse of heaven . . . who would have known what God would do this night?

All praise to our redeeming God. . . . Love's redeeming work was done, Hallelujah!

Was this the end at last? I looked across at my precious wife and children.

No, I thought, perhaps it's only just the beginning.

Postscript

The closing words of this book read, 'Was this the end at last? No, I thought, perhaps it's only just the beginning.' Little did Dave Cape realise how prophetic that thought was to be. The Cape family moved back to their home in Randburg, part of greater Johannesburg, looking forward to the prospect of a two-month break, simply relaxing and carrying out maintenance on their long-neglected home. Just before Christmas that same year however (December 1990), Dave again sensed the Lord speaking to him. While praying one evening he could clearly see a picture of Jesus standing crying over the tiny Middle East country of Kuwait. He sensed the Lord saying, 'I died for the Americans and the Iraqis; go and tell them that my love is impartial and that I died for them all.'

The upshot was that just a few weeks later Dave was winging his way to the Middle East, blissfully unaware that his obedience to the Spirit's promptings was to land him right in the middle of the soon-to-erupt Gulf War. His experiences there for almost the duration of the war are a story in themselves. But that is for another time and, perhaps, another book. Meanwhile, Dave's ministry continues as he carries the cross and bowl in different nations as well as ministering at conferences and preaching at churches. This unique prophetic statement of servanthood continues to touch both the poor and the powerful in Jesus' name.

Should you wish to get in touch with David Cape, his address is:
PO Box 48266,
Roosevelt Park,
Johannesburg, 2129,
Republic of South Africa.

Thanks

There are many who have played and who continue to play a vital part in the writing of this book and in all that the Lord has called me to do on earth. I give God thanks for those whom he has gathered around us as 'family' to declare the glory of our King Jesus. It is an honour to serve him with you. I just want to say I'm grateful to:

My mum and dad:
For first planting the seeds of my Saviour, the 'Life Giver' Jesus, in my heart. Also for your ever-faithful love and prayers.

Carol:
For being more than a wife, more than a mother, more than a woman, more than a friend. For being my 'covenant one-flesh' and for trusting the leading of the Holy Spirit within me, when many others doubted it. Experiencing your unwavering love is like living with Jesus.

Carynne and Ronald:
For your love and belief in me as your father. I trust that it will always also be so towards your heavenly Father. For allowing me the time to be away to tell others about Jesus.

Doug Laurie:
For 'getting inside me' to help me write this book. Your untiring enthusiasm, integrity and attention to detail have

overwhelmed me. It has been an honour to collaborate with you on this project.

Meryl Laurie:
My ever-faithful secretary. For the years that you have served Carol and me so faithfully, without ever complaining. For the hundreds and hundreds of letters you've typed over the years. For the hours and hours you've tirelessly laboured over the computer transcribing this manuscript.

Rex Currin:
For showing me Jesus and leading me to him.

Marc and Ann De Menzies:
For allowing me the use of your flat with its panoramic view of the Indian Ocean at Amanzimtoti to write the first part of this book.

Charles, Laura, Rob and Terry Charlewood/Spanjaard:
For the use of your tranquil cottage along the unspoilt coastline near Cape St Francis, to enable me to write the second part of this book.

Dad 'Pa' Faragher:
For keeping me company and for doing the cooking at Cape St Francis. Also for your constant encouragement to Carol, me and the children.

Eidur Adalgeirsson:
For being my precious 'servant-friend'.

Brian and Pauline Cape:
My beloved brother and sister, both naturally and in the Lord. It will be revealed only in heaven how you have loved, believed and supported in prayer the eternity that God has sown in my heart.

Ron and Ann Robinson, John and Gill Irving, Ashton and Grace Sparrow, Drummond and Linda Robinson and the rest of my family at Church of the Nations, Robinhills:
For your prayer, love, encouragement and support

starting long before this ever began to take place—I love you and Jesus in your midst.

Ron and Ann Robinson:
For always loving and believing in me, even at times when I may have given you cause to doubt.

Rob and Terry Spanjaard:
For your constant love, encouragement, support and sacrifice—above and beyond the call of friendship. Your love has spanned so many areas it would be impossible to list them all. We're exceedingly grateful for all you have done to make our calling a reality.

Richard Herkes:
Who first exhorted me to write this book. For your belief in me and your letters of encouragement when at times you must have wondered if it would ever happen.

The Bride of Christ:
Throughout Southern Africa and far beyond. For opening your sanctuaries, hearts, homes, finances and resources to us in ways too numerous to mention, ensuring that we are able to continue to show the servant-love of Jesus as we continue to carry the cross and bowl to the uttermost parts of the earth. Forgive me for not mentioning every member by name.

Gerry and Chris Armstrong, Sam and Ailsa Blundell, Tony and Marilyn Fitzgerald, Clive and Charmaine Soekoe and Peter and Lorna Trickey:
Thank you.

Ron and Sharon Faragher:
Precious brother and sister, we love you. Sharon for sparing Ron in the many hours he has spent reconstructing our caravans and turning them into home for us.

Most of all I want to thank the Lord Jesus Christ, my covenant keeper. For his grace, mercy and faithfulness. To my heavenly Father God for sending Jesus that by his resurrecting power I have been redeemed. That continually I may, even if falteringly, reflect his love.

Lord, make me more like you.